THE GREAT BOOK OF HORRIBLE FACTS

THE GREAT BOOK OF
HORRIBLE
FACTS

ARCTURUS

ARCTURUS

This edition published in 2013 by Arcturus Publishing Limited
26/27 Bickels Yard, 151–153 Bermondsey Street,
London SE1 3HA

ISBN: 978-1-78212-428-3
CH001871EN

Authors: Anne Rooney and Helen Otway
Editor: Rebecca Gerlings
Cover illustration by Dynamo Design

Supplier 24, Date 0713, Print Run 2651

Printed in Malaysia

CONTENTS

SOME horrible Facts

PASS THE BUCKET...

Even if you can boast a gross little brother or sister who picks their nose or farts in your sleeping bag, believe it or not there are things going on right now all over the world that are far, far yuckier than that. Fully grown adults who should know better do some really horrible things, too.

For instance, did you know that in some places people don't let their dead rest in peace, keeping them up all hours (and years) joining in family celebrations? Or that in other places people eat rotten food – and not because they forgot to go to the shops, but because they actually *like* it? Did you know that some animals eat their dinner while it's still alive? And do you know what's living in your body – apart from you? Would you like to find out? Then this is the book for you!

Try to have a bucket handy – or you could pick up some sickness bags next time you go on a ship or a plane.

Facts about airsickness bags:

Virgin Atlantic got top designers to work on its airsickness bags. The cost of a full set of 20 stylish bags has been known to reach triple figures.

You can buy rare airsickness bags on eBay.

The world's largest collection of airsickness bags is owned by Niek Vermeulen of the Netherlands, who has 3,728 of them, from 802 airlines.

A British Airways airsickness bag from 1996 has instructions (for what? vomiting?) in 11 languages – which is a record, apparently.

There is an email group for people who want to swap (unused) airsickness bags.

Over to you

If you make it to the end of this book without keeling over, well done! Next time you see your brother eating his earwax or see something gross on TV – like the man who had a snake living in his gut for years without realising why he always felt so hungry – you might not feel quite so disgusted.

Now, ready to cringe?
Then read on...

Don't try this at home!

There are some pretty yucky things in this book. In fact, some are world records in grossness. But that doesn't mean you should try to out-gross them yourself. Some are actually rather dangerous, and people have spent years training themselves to do them. Can you *imagine* training for years to hang from your earlobes or gobble snails? Why would you? Get a life! More importantly, keep the life you've got! If you happen to find yourself burping nonstop for 90 years or growing an eyebrow as long as a battleship, get in touch with the *Guinness Book of World Records*. Otherwise, leave it to the experts.

Horrible Body Facts

Florida woman Gayle Grinds was so obese that after spending six years on her couch, her skin became fused to the upholstery.

Nose mucus is normally clear. But if you have a bacterial infection it turns yellow, or even green!

Your appendix looks like a worm dangling from your intestine... and you don't even need it for anything!

Even though your gastric juices are highly acidic, they cannot digest chewing gum. A small piece of gum will pass right through the digestive system, but larger amounts can cause a serious blockage.

There are 250,000 sweat glands in your feet, all working away to make sure your socks smell really cheesy!

If an astronaut burps, it is a sick burp; the lack of gravity means any food is floating about at the top of the stomach!

Your nose produces a cup of mucus each day. Would you like some cake with that?

Early x-rays caused nasty side effects such as skin burns, swelling and hair loss.

Spanish artist Salvador Dalí used to study his stools and make notes on their colour and consistency.

The skin you can see on your body is dead! New cells are growing underneath to give you a new layer of skin every 30 days.

Quinsy, a complication of tonsillitis, is a putrid abscess in the throat. The sufferer will drool rather than endure the agony of swallowing their saliva.

Australian Graham Barker has been collecting his own belly button fluff every day since 1984 and keeps it in storage jars.

Women of the Himalayan Apatani tribe used to enlarge their nostrils with circular, 2.5 centimetres (1 inch) wide nose plugs.

The condition of excessive body hair is called *hypertrichosis,* or Werewolf Syndrome.

When you crack your knuckles, the noise comes from gas bubbles popping in the liquid around your joints.

A carbuncle is a large abscess on the skin that oozes pus from one or two holes.

Native American man Dennis Avner, otherwise known as Stalking Cat, has gone to great lengths to be tigrine: he has stripes tattooed on his body, his ears have been surgically elongated and he inserts synthetic whiskers into facial piercings.

Devoted Hindus attending the Malaysian Thaipusam festival stick skewers through their skin as part of the celebrations.

Each year, 6,500 people are taken to British hospitals after being injured by a lawnmower. Injuries include the slicing off of a toe or even a finger!

Indian man Vijayakanth can pass a thread through his tear duct and out through his mouth in just 60 seconds.

Blood whizzes through the main artery in the body, the *aorta*, at 30 centimetres (12 inches) a second. If the aorta is cut, imagine how fast the blood spurts out!

The first time you get a cold sore, the virus that causes it lurks in your body for the rest of your life.

You've got jelly in your bones! It is called *bone marrow* and it makes your blood cells.

Dutch artist Joanneke Meester had a section of skin surgically removed from her abdomen and used it to make a replica pistol as a comment on rising violence.

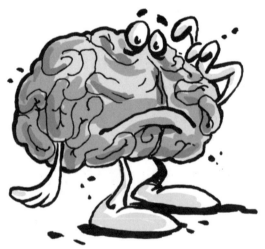

Whilst playing for Swiss team Servette, Portuguese soccer player Paulo Diogo tried to jump over a metal barrier during a goal celebration. His wedding ring got caught and he lost the top half of his finger. He even got a yellow card for wasting time!

The body uses 16 different chemicals to create a scab.

A person struck by lightning may have red, snaky patterns on their skin afterwards. These are known as *Lichtenberg figures* or *lightning flowers* and are caused by ruptured blood capillaries.

After being removed from the body, the lungs can survive longer than any other organ.

The *cornea* (the surface of your eye) is the only part of your body that has no blood supply. It is still not a good idea to cut it, though.

You have bones in your body that are not attached to any other bone. These 'floating' bones are your triangular kneecaps and the horseshoe-shaped *hyoid* in your neck.

Bits of dried earwax come loose and fall out when you chew, yawn or swallow!

Ninety per cent of the hairs on your head are growing at any point during the day. The other 10 per cent are just having a rest!

The sound of a burp is caused by the vibration of the *cardia* (where your stomach and oesophagus meet) when gas from your stomach whizzes through it. More gas means a louder burp.

Emetophobia **is a fear of vomiting.**

The heart pumps blood around your body with enough pressure to squirt it 9 metres (30 feet) away.

One symptom of scarlet fever is strawberry tongue – the tongue swells up and turns bright red, making it look like a strawberry.

American surgeon William Beaumont researched human digestion by putting pieces of food on string and poking them through an old gunshot wound in an ex-patient's stomach. He pulled out the food at intervals to see the effects of digestion on it.

Pellagra is a vitamin deficiency disease caused by lack of protein and vitamin B. In severe cases, it is characterized by 'the four d's': diarrhoea, dermatitis, dementia and death.

Maggots have been used for thousands of years to help clean and heal wounds, as they munch away at dead flesh. Some really greedy maggots eat the other maggots too.

Malaria is caused by parasites in the saliva of mosquitoes that get into the human bloodstream. The parasites multiply in the liver and red blood cells.

The temperature of your farts is around 37 degrees Celsius (98.6 degrees Fahrenheit), the same as your body. They might feel hotter if you've eaten something spicy.

Depending on the infection, pus can be white, yellow, brown or blue. Yes, blue!

A Mexican man made a protest against the discrimination of people with tattoos and piercings by putting hooks through his back and arms, using them to dangle himself from a tree.

Short-sighted people have bigger eyeballs than those who are long-sighted.

Wealthy Texan recluse Howard Hughes was so obsessed with protecting his body from germs that he could not use a spoon unless his staff had first covered the handle in layers of tissue paper and cellophane.

You can hear the blood flowing through your ears if you find a quiet place and cover them tightly.

Someone with *cutaneous anthrax* will have large, black ulcers on their skin.

American multi-millionairess Hetty Green was so stingy that she would not pay for her son to have his broken leg treated. He then got gangrene and had to have the limb amputated.

Stick your tongue out! Those bumps on it are called *papillae* and they contain your taste buds. You were born with 10,000 taste buds but they die with age, so your grandparents may have only 5,000.

The skin is the body's largest organ. If you lay it out and smooth out the wrinkles, it can cover an area of up to 2 square metres (7 square feet).

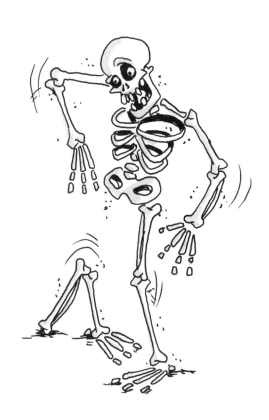

Members of the Native American Mandan tribe used to keep the skulls of their dead and place them in a circle formation near their village.

Bowel obstruction (a blocked bowel) can lead to faecal vomiting, in which faeces are expelled back into the stomach from the colon and up through the mouth.

Keraunoparalysis is the temporary paralysis of the legs suffered after being struck by lightning.

In 2004, Uruguayan artist Carlos Capelán exhibited collages made from toenail clippings.

British man Richard Ross inhaled a nail that he was holding between his lips whilst doing DIY in his home. His ribs had to be broken for the subsequent lung surgery to remove it and he spent three weeks in hospital.

Nail files can carry nail fungus, bacteria and viruses.

If the body is fighting an infection, the *lymph nodes* can swell to the size of an orange. We call them 'swollen glands'.

The reclusive Collyer brothers' Harlem house was so full of junk that after Homer Collyer died, police and workmen cleared rubbish for two weeks before they found the body of his brother, Langley.

18th-century footmen, who had to walk closely behind their masters or mistresses, were known colloquially as 'fart-catchers'.

When gas escapes from a dead body, it sounds like the corpse is farting.

One of the first stages of embalming a dead body is called 'setting the features', which includes stitching or gluing the lips together to keep the mouth shut.

An old remedy for warts used to be to rub a piece of raw meat on them and then bury the meat. It was thought that as the meat rotted away, the warts would disappear.

Tinea cruris is a fungal infection of the groin area. Sufferers are often sportspeople, so it's commonly known as 'jock itch'!

Queen Elizabeth I had black teeth. Like most Elizabethans, she was fond of sugary foods but toothbrushes and toothpaste hadn't yet been invented.

Obstipation is severe constipation. If it lasts for days, it can cause bloating, distention and terrible pain.

The deadly poison *strychnine* has a dramatic effect on the body – all the muscles go into spasm, causing convulsions until the back arches and breathing stops. *Rigor mortis* (stiffening) sets in immediately, with the eyes remaining wide open.

Verrucas that grow in clusters are known as *mosaic warts*.

Clubbing is a condition that causes the hands to swell up and makes the fingers look like fat sausages. It is caused by liver malfunction.

After scoring the winning goal against Ecuador in a 2006 World Cup match, England captain David Beckham vomited on the pitch.

If your breath is a bit stinky in the morning, it's because your saliva glands have slowed down while you were asleep, making your mouth dry. It doesn't take long for them to get back into action again.

Argentinian artist Nicola Constantino has made 100 soaps and two sculptures from her own fat! The fat was removed from her body using liposuction.

A *teratoma*, meaning 'monster tumour', is a rare growth inside the body that can have hair and teeth.

A stool that floats and won't flush away is full of gas.

Scurvy used to be a common condition caused by vitamin C deficiency. It would cause spongy gums, loose teeth, purple blotches on the skin and, in extreme cases, death. Anyone for an orange?

Eating lots of beetroot will make your urine pink.

During a severe nosebleed, blood can travel up the sinuses and come out through the eyes.

If you ever jump as if you're being electrocuted when drifting off to sleep, you're experiencing a *hypnic jerk*. The brain mistakes pre-sleep relaxation for falling and stiffens the limbs to get the body upright again.

American surfer Bethany Hamilton had her left arm bitten off by a tiger shark but went back to surfing just ten weeks later.

First World War soldiers often suffered from *trench mouth*, in which the gums would swell up and bleed, becoming covered in ulcers. Left untreated, it spread to the cheeks and lips.

Your teeth are soft in the middle! The outside is made of *enamel*, which is the hardest substance in your body. Inside is squidgy stuff called *pulp*, made of nerves, blood vessels and tissue.

Stale urine used to be an ingredient in gunpowder.

Amongst the 103 tonnes of junk removed from the Collyer brothers' house in Harlem were human organs pickled in jars and a horse's jawbone.

A liver with *cirrhosis* is an orangey yellow colour and lumpy.

The deadly *Ebola* virus makes sufferers throw up thick, black vomit.

Guinea worm disease is caught from drinking infected water in tropical countries. Between one and two years after infection, a spaghetti-like worm up to 100 centimetres (40 inches) long will pop out of a blister in the foot or leg.

A person who has had an eye removed can suffer from *phantom eye syndrome*; they experience sensations, pain and hallucinations in the missing eye.

Eating potent foods such as chillies and garlic will make your sweat smell stronger.

Tooth decay has been around for thousands of years and in ancient times was believed to have been caused by a 'tooth worm'.

Major aphthous ulcerations are mouth ulcers that are more than a centimetre (half an inch) wide. Ouch!

The part of your brain that controls body stuff like vomiting and salivating is called the *medulla*.

Not all dead bodies decompose after burial. If conditions are right, the skin develops a soapy coating called *adipocere* and the body becomes naturally mummified.

One day's worth of your farts is enough to blow up a small balloon.

Squatting is the best position for the body to be in when passing a stool.

If you eat ice cream too quickly, the blood vessels in your head swell up and give you a 'brain freeze' headache. Your nerves send messages to the brain that you're in a cold environment, so the blood vessels swell to warm you up.

Spanish artist Francisco de Goya got lead poisoning from the paints he used and became completely deaf.

Blood is made up of 92 per cent water.

American mountaineer Aron Ralston had to take drastic action when a boulder fell on his arm and pinned him to the ground in Blue John Canyon, Utah. After five days, desperation drove him to amputate the arm with a penknife.

Queen Elizabeth I was so afraid of having one of her rotten teeth extracted that a loyal Archbishop had to have one of his teeth out first to reassure her.

Going up a mountain too quickly will make you vomit! At heights over 2,500 metres (8,000 feet) above sea level, a change in pressure means the body does not get as much oxygen and needs time to acclimatize. If not, altitude sickness will occur.

If you have a cut in your skin, it takes less than 10 seconds for your blood to start clotting to form a scab.

Just like your fingerprints, your tongue print is unique – it's just a bit sloppier!

When Polish man Hubert Hoffman criticized the country's president Lech Kaczynski during a routine police check, he was asked to show more respect. He replied with a loud fart and was promptly arrested!

A 19th-century cure for toothache was to hammer a nail into the tooth and then stick the nail in a tree to transfer the pain.

Cauliflower ear is caused by blood clots forming on the ear after being hit or by skin being torn from the ear's cartilage, making ugly lumps and bumps. Boxers often suffer from this, but it's probably best not to point it out if you meet one!

Inventors Michael Zanakis and Philip Femano patented a fart-powered toy rocket in 2005.

Eating asparagus produces a chemical called *methanethiol* that makes urine smell of rotten cabbage.

19th-century English footballer Joe Powell broke his arm so badly during a match that he got *tetanus* and blood poisoning as a result. His arm was amputated in an attempt to save him, but he died a week later.

The world's most pierced woman, Elaine Davidson, can put her little finger through the hole in her tongue.

If your skin did not secrete its naturally antibacterial substances, you would go mouldy!

Hair cannot turn white with fright, but shock can make pigmented hair suddenly fall out. An older person whose hair is a mixture of colour and grey would then be left with only grey hairs, appearing to turn white overnight.

The rare but fatal brain disease *kuru* is also known as laughing sickness, as its victims go through a stage of bursting into laughter, before they develop ulcerations and eventually die.

NASA aeroplanes used for training astronauts have the nickname 'Vomit Comets', as the weightlessness that passengers experience often makes them throw up.

Characteristics of tetanus are muscle spasms in the jaw and difficulty swallowing, which is why the disease is also known as 'lockjaw'.

Indian man Dharmendra Singh can make cigarette smoke come out of his ears. He can whistle through his nose too!

By the time of her death, Queen Elizabeth I's coronation ring had become embedded in her flesh. The ring had to be sawn off so that it could be passed to the heir to the throne, James VI of Scotland.

Sufferers of *blackwater fever* pass black urine, hence the name.

Brain diseases known as *spongiform encephalopathies* cause the brain to become riddled with holes.

The blood vessels in the *conjunctiva* (eye membrane) are very fragile. If ruptured, a bright red haemorrhage will spread across the white of the eye.

Italian artist Piero Manzoni filled 90 small tins with his own faeces for a 1961 exhibition. Some of them later exploded!

Indian painter Shihan Hussaini used over a litre of his blood to paint 56 portraits of politician Jayalalitha for her 56th birthday.

Tendons attach your muscles to your bones and look like rubber bands. Like rubber bands, they can also snap.

After a car accident in Nottinghamshire, England, a back seat passenger was impaled by a snooker cue that had been in the car's boot. It missed her vital organs and she was released from hospital after only three days.

Turkish construction worker Ilker Yilmaz can snort milk up his nose and squirt it more than 2.5 metres (9 feet)… from his eye!

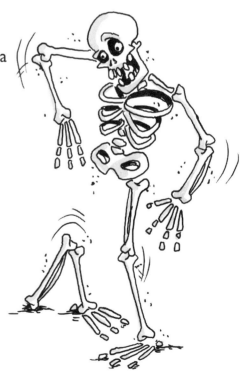

St Louis barber Bill Black used the hair clippings swept from his floor to make vests, shirts, ties and even a bikini!

When Canadian man Jim Sulkers died in his bed, his body was not discovered until two years later. The corpse had not decomposed but had become mummified in the hot, dry conditions at the time of his death.

Helmintophobia is a fear of being infested with worms. Who wouldn't be scared?

American man Matt Gone was so unhappy with his birthmarks that he has had 94 per cent of his body covered in a checkerboard tattoo.

Three million of your red blood cells die each second! Luckily, your body is replacing them just as quickly – one drop of your blood contains five million red blood cells.

A blister contains lymph and other body fluids. This is what makes them squidgy and tempting to pop!

There are more than 200 species of bacteria living on your skin at any one time. Some are good bacteria that are making themselves useful!

Joseph Merrick, known as 'The Elephant Man', suffered from a rare condition called *Proteus syndrome*, which causes disfiguring skin and bone growths.

Breckenridge carpenter Patrick Lawler suffered eye swelling and toothache after his nail gun backfired and a nail struck his face. When he had an x-ray six days later, it showed a second 10 centimetre (4 inch) nail embedded in his skull!

Some contortionists dislocate their hip or shoulder joints during their displays.

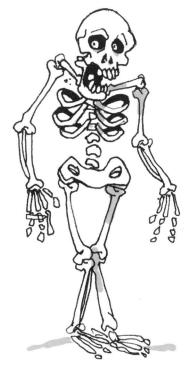

Sylvester the 'Cowboy Mummy' is displayed at Ye Olde Curiosity Shoppe in Seattle. Complete with gunshot wounds, he is preserved in arsenic, commonly used in the 19th century to preserve corpses.

A person who has been struck by lightning may have perforated eardrums, cataracts, burns or permanent brain damage as a result.

Intestinal myiasis is a condition where maggots are in a person's stomach. The maggots can be swallowed in infected food and cause cramps, but are eventually digested by gastric juices.

In 2004, Dutch eye surgeons invented eyeball jewellery; the eye membrane is sliced and a decorative shape is inserted. UK and US eye specialists have criticized the practice, since it could cause infection and scarring.

The black dot in the middle of a verruca is its blood supply.

American politician Stan Jones suffered from a condition called *argyria* after taking medicine that contained silver. His skin became permanently grey!

A *nasal polyp* is a fleshy growth in the nostril that can be as big as a grape.

The African tumbu fly lays its eggs in clothes. When the clothes are worn, the eggs hatch and the larvae burrow into the skin, creating boil-like sores for the maggots to grow in.

An average appendix is 10 centimetres (3.94 inches) long. The longest appendix ever removed came from a man in Pakistan: it was 23.5 centimetres (9 inches) long!

You had more than 300 bones when you were born, but by the time you're an adult you'll have only 206! Don't worry, you won't lose them – some of your bones will just fuse together.

When British footballer Darius Vassell had a blood blister under his toenail, he tried to get rid of it… by drilling a hole in the nail himself! His DIY surgery led to an infection and the loss of half his toenail.

Entropion
is a condition in which the eyelid turns inwards against the eyeball. The skin rubs against the surface of the eyeball and can cause sight loss.

British performance artist Mark McGowan spent two weeks sitting on a London street with his raised arm strapped to a lamppost, draining the blood from his arm and possibly causing muscle damage. He called this anti-war protest *The Withered Arm*.

All your bodily functions stop when you sneeze… even your heartbeat!

Catgut, used for stitching cuts, is made from sheep or goat intestines.

Fijian rugby player Jone Tawake decided to have his right ring finger amputated when a dislocated joint became infected.

In 1970, a thief was caught in Zurich, Switzerland, when a finger that had been cut off by broken glass at the crime scene was matched to his fingerprints in police records.

Girls who made matches in the 1800s often suffered from 'phossy jaw' – their jawbones would rot away, poisoned by the phosphorus used to make the matches.

The average person loses 200 millilitres (7 fluid ounces) of water a day in their faeces.

The maw worm can grow to 30 centimetres (1 foot) and then come out of the body from any gap or hole, including the corner of the eye.

You turn white when you're really scared because blood drains from your skin. This protected primitive humans from bleeding to death if bitten by scary, wild animals.

More than 200 types of different organisms live inside or on your body at any time.

In 1973, Italian kidnappers were paid a ransom of over $3 million after they cut off the ear of their kidnap victim and sent it to his very rich grandfather, John Paul Getty.

All the bacteria living inside your body would fill six teaspoons.

If you could scrunch together all the bacteria living on the outside of your body, they would take up about the same amount of space as one pea.

Long ago, rich people used to pay for teeth to be pulled from poor people – often teenagers – and implanted in their own jaws when their rotten teeth were removed.

If your vomit looks like what you've just eaten, that's exactly what it is. If it's soupy, then it's because it's been in your stomach for a while.

Pinworms cause an itchy bottom because they sneak out at night to lay their eggs there.

Ten billion scales of skin fall off your body every day.

When diarrhoea turns pale, it contains bits of the lining of your gut.

Urine doesn't contain bacteria. Becalmed or shipwrecked sailors who had run out of fresh water used to drink it with no ill effects.

Dentists in the Far East used to pull teeth out with their bare hands! In China, they practised by pulling nails out of wood with their fingers.

Your body needs sleep. Staying awake for two weeks can be enough to kill you.

Adult feet produce about a quarter of a cup of sweat a day from 250,000 pores – wait four days and you could make a cup of foot sweat tea!

Foods that will make you fart include beans, bran, broccoli, sprouts, cabbage, cauliflower and onions.

The larvae of the pork tapeworm, hatched from eggs eaten in infected pork, can travel around the body and live in the brain, eyes, heart or muscles.

At least 1.3 billion people are infected with a small hookworm that attaches to the inside of the gut. If there are a lot, it looks like fur or a thick carpet. Around the world, they suck a total of 10 million litres (around 21 million pints) of blood a day.

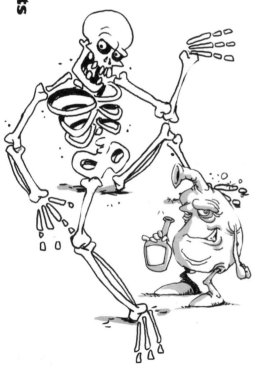

An Indian man known as Snake Manu can put small snakes, including deadly cobras, into his mouth and pass them out through his nose.

In ancient Mexico, people bound their babies' heads tightly to make their skulls long and thin.

Surma girls of Ethiopia put clay disks in their lower lip, stretching the lip outwards. The size of the disk indicates how many cattle a man needs to provide to marry the girl – they can be up to 15 centimetres (6 inches) across.

When a wound gets infected, it oozes yellow pus. Pus is a mixture of dead blood cells, bacteria and other dead cells from your body.

Prickly heat rash is caused by sweat sticking to the layer of dead skin cells on top of your skin. As the cells can't fall off, the sweat can't escape and makes the live cells underneath swell up.

Most people have mites – very tiny creatures that are related to spiders – living in their eyelashes, eyebrows, ears and noses.

For a work entitled *Self*, created in 1991, English sculptor Marc Quinn made a copy of his head, moulded from his own deep-frozen blood. Quinn collected almost 4 litres (8 pints) of his blood over five months, poured it into a mould of his head and froze it.

About 70 millilitres (around 2.5 fluid ounces) of blood are spurted out of your heart with each beat.

The *Wucheria* worm can live in the lymph system and grow up to 12 centimetres (5 inches) long.

About a third of your faeces is not old food, but bacteria that help you to digest food, and bits of the lining of the inside of your gut.

In some countries, the umbilical cord – the cord that attaches the unborn baby to its mother – is dried and kept after birth, to use in spells or medicines.

In some parts of Africa and on some Pacific islands, people make patterns of raised scars on their skin as a decoration or to show their bravery. The wounds are made with sharp spikes or thorns from plants and often rubbed with special kinds of earth or leaves to created coloured tattoos.

Pilgrims to the Tirupati temple in India give some of their hair as a sacrifice. The temple employs 600 barbers who work day and night to shave pilgrims, taking 6.5 million gifts of hair a year. The hair is sold to wig makers and for use as fertilizer.

People who lose an arm or leg in an accident or operation can often still feel it hurting, aching or itching but can do nothing to make it feel better.

> **Dust mites are found in all houses. They eat the dead skin we shed all the time, and live in beds, carpets, rugs and anywhere else snug which collects flakes of skin.**

If you unravelled all the tiny tubes in your kidneys and laid them end to end, they would stretch 80 kilometres (50 miles). Yet they scrunch up to fit into kidneys only 10 centimetres (4 inches) long.

> **An *amoeba* common in warm water can travel up your nose while you are swimming and live in your brain, where it multiplies rapidly and kills you in three to seven days.**

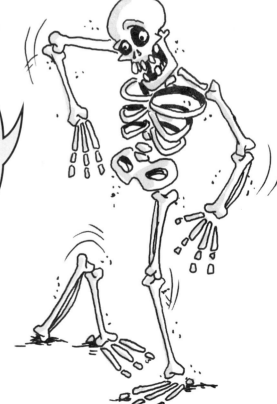

You will produce 45,000 litres (around 95,000 pints) of urine in your life – enough to fill a small swimming pool!

The old Chinese medical technique of acupuncture involves sticking lots of very thin needles into a person's body. The theory is that putting the needles on 'energy pathways' around the body relieves pain and cures illness.

Head lice can change colour to merge in with the hair they are hiding in.

Urine is a good remedy for jellyfish stings, so if you're standing in the sea and get stung, just urinate down your legs.

Liposuction is a popular operation in Europe and the USA amongst people who feel they are too fat. A surgeon sticks a long, hollow needle into the fat part – such as the tummy or thighs – uses ultrasound to turn the fat to yellow mush, and then sucks it out through the needle.

Athlete's foot is a fungus that grows in the warm, sweaty spaces between your toes. It causes itching and split skin.

The palms of the hands are the sweatiest parts of the body, followed by the feet.

When ancient Egyptians mummified someone, they used a special long-handled spoon to scoop the brains out through the dead person's nose. They often fed the brains to animals.

If you don't brush plaque off your teeth, it hardens into a substance called *tartar* which is like cement and impossible to remove with your toothbrush.

The medical name for earwax is *cerumen*; it is produced by more than 4,000 glands in your ears.

It's possible to get dandruff in your eyebrows as well as in the hair on top of your head.

Chewing gum and using straws both make you burp more as they encourage you to swallow air.

A facelift to remove wrinkles involves cutting away part of the skin, pulling the remainder tight again and stitching it in place.

Some people have injections of collagen to 'plump up' their wrinkles. The collagen – a fibre found in skin – is usually taken from pigs or cows.

If you never wear shoes, the skin on the soles of your feet eventually thickens and hardens so that you can walk over sharp stones without hurting yourself.

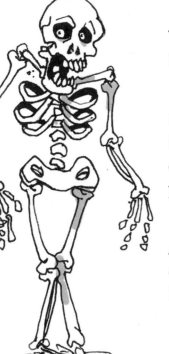

The Bedouin people in the Middle East consider it polite to burp after a meal.

Hair grows all over your body except the palms of your hands, soles of your feet and your lips.

A single drop of blood contains 250 million blood cells.

Vomiting a lot can give you a black eye – the pressure can burst the blood vessels around your eyes.

Romans used to clean their teeth with urine, and it was used as a mouthwash until the 1800s in Europe.

A bruise is bleeding under your skin. The blood can't get out if there isn't a cut, so it just leaks around – it's purple because that's the colour of blood that doesn't have any oxygen in it.

Even a bald person has very fine hair on their head, called *vellus*.

The gunge that collects in your belly button is a mix of dirt, dead skin cells and oils from your body.

If you could line up all your blood cells – all 25 billion of them – they would go round the world four times.

The Binderwur tribe in India used to kill and eat sick and old people to please their goddess Kali.

The medical name for burping is *eructation*.

Your belly button is formed from the shrivelled up stump of the umbilical cord – the tube that connected you to your mother's body before you were born.

Over a ton of pubic hair has to be filtered out of London's sewage each year and removed to landfill sites.

Most people fart about 14 times a day.

A very fat person who flushes an aeroplane toilet while still sitting on it can have their rectum sucked out by the pull of the toilet's flush.

At any one time, parasites account for one-hundredth of your body weight.

Human hair grows about just over a centimetre (half an inch) a month.

Air you swallow, and gas released from food as you digest it, comes out as a burp or a fart – which one depends on how far through your intestines it has got.

The best recorded distance for projectile vomiting is 8 metres (27 feet)!

Expert botfly squeezers (employed to remove botfly maggots from people) can shoot a botfly from an infected swelling distances of 3 metres (10 feet) or more.

When you die, the bacteria in your gut start to eat away at you from the inside.

The botfly lays its eggs on a mosquito, and they hatch when the mosquito bites someone. The maggot grows for six weeks in a lump under the person's skin called a warble until it pops out when it's fully grown.

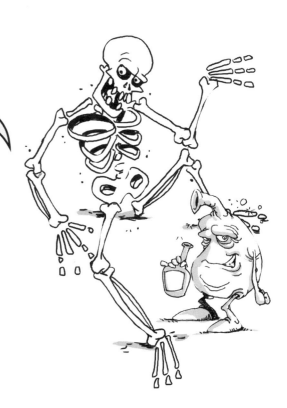

A man with the stage name of Enigma has had surgery to give him horns on his head. He's hoping to get a tail sometime in the future.

In some parts of the world, people wear extremely heavy earrings to weigh their ears down and stretch the lobes. They can weigh up to half a kilogram (1 pound) and hang from huge, long holes in the earlobe.

You swallow about 1 litre (2 pints) of mucus every day.

Rhinotillexomania is the scientific word for picking your nose.

When you breathe normally, air goes into your nose at about 6.5 kilometres (4 miles) per hour. When you take a good sniff at something, it goes in at 32 kilometres (20 miles) per hour. When you sneeze, it comes out at 160 kilometres (100 miles) per hour!

A scab forms because cells in your blood called platelets make a very thin fibre that traps other blood cells and holds them in a layer that dries out over a scratch or cut.

If you could lay out all your blood vessels end to end, they would go more than twice round the world.

The mental disorder called 'walking corpse' disease leads people to believe parts of their body are missing or that they are dead.

There is enough iron in the human body to make a nail.

Your body absorbs about two-thirds of the volume of the food you eat – the rest is squished into faeces.

Hookworms can infest people who walk barefoot. They bore through the skin of the feet and travel in the blood to the lungs, where they come out and crawl up to the throat, to be swallowed and start a new life in the gut.

A dead body quickly looks greyish as the blood drains down to the part of the body closest to the ground. The effect is most noticeable in people with white skin.

Right-handed people sweat most under their right arm, left-handed people sweat most under their left arm.

People who live in big cities make more earwax than those who live in the country, where the air is cleaner.

Nearly half of the dust in your house – and what's sucked up when you vacuum the house – consists of old skin cells!

Your intestines are about four times your height – they fit because they're all squashed up and coiled around.

An adult has around 5 million hairs on their head and body.

The infection *thrush* causes a white, hairy fungus to grow on the tongue.

Nose-pickings are a mix of drying mucus and rubbish filtered out of the air you breathe in – pollen, dust, smoke, dirt, sand, and even tiny particles of dust from space!

The skin of an adult laid out flat on the floor would cover about 1.67 square metres (18 square feet).

Dandruff is a mixture of dirt and dead skin cells stuck together with oil that oozes out of your glands on your head. If your head oozes too much oil, your dandruff becomes noticeable.

Babies can get extra thick, yellow dandruff that sticks to their heads in scales. It's called *cradle cap* and is more noticeable because they usually don't have much hair.

The toilet paper that Americans use in one day would go around the world nine times.

A person produces 1.5 litres (2.6 pints) of spit (saliva) every day and swallows almost all of it.

You lose 80 hairs from your head every day – but you have about 100,000 so don't worry, you won't start to look bald just yet. And they regrow quickly when you're young.

Your heart pumps around 182 million litres (48 million gallons) of blood in your lifetime – with an endless supply of blood, it could fill a swimming pool in less than a month!

Beards grow faster than any other body hair. If a man never cut his beard, it would grow 9.1 metres (30 feet) in his lifetime.

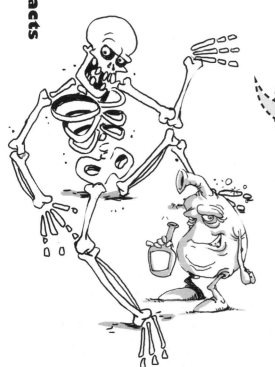

If you could spread out your lungs on the ground, unravelling all the tiny little pockets, they would cover a tennis court.

Being born is really stressful! As you came into the world, you had higher levels of the stress hormone adrenaline in your body than an adult would during a heart attack.

When you blush, your stomach blushes too! A blush sends blood flooding into the tiny blood vessels on your face and also to the many blood vessels inside your stomach.

The longest tapeworm ever found in a human was 33 metres (around 108 feet) long.

When you vomit, the same muscle movements that push food down through your gut go into reverse, pushing it back up again.

Between entering your mouth and coming out of your bottom, it can take up to two days for food to pass through your body.

A spot or pimple is caused by a waxy oil called *sebum* and tiny bits of dead skin collecting in a little hole in your skin. It turns black if it gets big enough to force your pore open and let air in. When bacteria start to eat away at the gunk, a red spot with nasty yellow pus inside grows.

One in 100,000 people is born with an extra finger on each hand, but usually they are only small stumps.

Roundworm is the most common gut parasite in the world. It looks rather like an earthworm, and you can catch it by eating food contaminated with faeces.

If you could remove your brain and spread it out, it would be the size of a pillowcase.

A smelly fart contains the same gas that makes rotten eggs stink – *hydrogen sulphide*.

If too much wax builds up in your ears, a doctor can soften it and then scoop it out with a special spoon called a *curette*.

Danish astronomer Tyco Brahe wore a metal nose because his own fell off after he suffered from the disease *syphilis*.

Sometimes, if a person's eye comes out of its socket in an accident and dangles on their cheek, they can push it back in with no lasting ill effects – don't try it at home!

When you sleep, you aren't blinking so there is no way to sweep away the mix of water, oils and other chemicals that wash over your eyes. Instead, they dry out around the edges of your eyes making crispy or slimy yellow gunk.

Sweat doesn't actually smell – it's the bacteria breaking it down that produce the pong.

One in 600 people are born with kidneys that are fused together in a horseshoe shape.

Wet hair stretches to about 1.5 times its dry length.

The sores caused by the disease *typhus* can rot the flesh, sometimes causing toes and fingers to drop off.

If you took all the nerves out of an adult's body and laid them end to end, they would stretch 75 kilometres (47 miles). But the adult would not be pleased.

Men grow ear hair as they get older; women don't.

Food can slosh around in your stomach for up to 4 hours, churning around like a washing machine.

Feet smell really bad sometimes because lots of bacteria and fungi like to live on them – especially if they are hot and wet and sweaty. The bacteria feed on the dead skin and sweat making smelly gases.

If you have a spitting contest, you'll do better if you can see some food, or even a picture of food. If you can't manage that, just thinking about your favourite food will help to make your mouth water.

If you throw up and your vomit is greenish, it contains bile from further down in your intestine than just your stomach. The bile and stomach acid make vomit taste awful.

The disease *necrotising fasciitis* causes the flesh to rot from within and drop off in chunks. Holes up to 15 centimetres (6 inches) across can form in sufferers' bodies.

Your eyes make 4.5 litres (8 pints) of tears a year – they keep your eyes wet even if you're not crying.

Slime oozes from the inside of your stomach to stop the acid in the stomach dissolving its walls and eating into your body – digesting you from the inside.

A gut parasite carried in water infested half a million people in Wisconsin in 1993 when it got into the water supply. A hundred people died.

Stomach gurgling – called *borborygmus* by scientists – is the sound of half-digested food, gas and stomach acid churning around inside.

After you die, your body starts to dry out and shrink, creating the illusion that your hair and nails are still growing after death.

If you are close to a really loud noise – a massive volcano erupting, or a huge explosion – the thin, tight skin inside your ear called your eardrum can burst with the pressure.

To save space, 98 per cent of dead Japanese people are cremated rather than buried.

There are more germs under your fingernails than on a toilet seat.

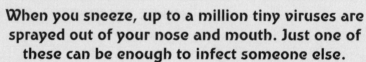

When you sneeze, up to a million tiny viruses are sprayed out of your nose and mouth. Just one of these can be enough to infect someone else.

Babies are born without kneecaps – they develop at between two to six years of age.

In Palestine, pregnant women who hoped for a son used to drink a potion made from the burned and powdered umbilical cord of a newborn baby boy.

Urine doesn't smell until it hits the air. Then a chemical in it called *urea* starts to break down into *ammonia* and the smell begins…

Chinese leader Mao Tse Tung never brushed his teeth, giving as a reason that tigers never brushed their teeth either.

William McIloy had 400 operations because he suffered from Munchausen's Syndrome, which is a mental disorder that makes people want to receive medical treatment. He had to give a false name and move around a lot to get away with it.

People either have pale and dry or dark and sticky earwax. It's an inherited trait, with dry earwax more common in Asia or people of Asian decent.

Faeces smell largely because the microbes in your gut produce two stinky chemicals as they work to break down your food – *indole* and *skatole*.

Two thousand glands in your ear make earwax to protect you from getting dirt, dust and germs deep in your ear. The wax slowly hardens and comes to the edge of your ear to fall out. If it doesn't fall out, it can harden into a plug of wax up to 2.5 centimetres (about 1 inch) long.

> **Before artificial false teeth were made of porcelain in the 1800s, many people who needed false teeth wore teeth pulled from the mouths of corpses.**

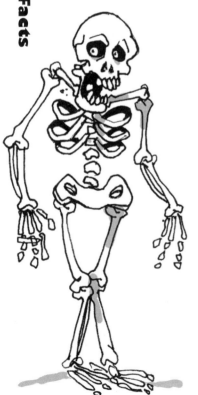

The weight of ashes from the average cremated human body is 4 kilograms (9 pounds).

King Louis IV of France had a stomach twice the size of a normal human stomach.

> **A French entertainer in the late 1800s used to make 'music' by farting out tunes.**

A man with the stage name Lizardman has slit his tongue in two, from the tip to the middle, so that it's forked. He also has green scales tattooed over his skin.

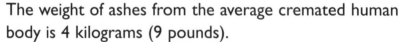

You shed and regrow your skin roughly every 27 days, making a total of around 1,000 complete skins in a lifetime. A person who lives to 70 years of age will shed 47.6 kilograms (105 pounds) of skin.

A newborn baby produces its own body weight in faeces every 60 hours.

It takes just over 3 kilograms (7 pounds) of pressure to tear off a human ear – don't try it!

King Louis XIV of France's feet started to rot in old age. A valet found a toe that had dropped off in one of the king's socks.

There is enough fat in the human body to make seven bars of soap.

When you have diarrhoea, instead of absorbing water from your food, your intestines ooze more water into it to rush it through the system and out the other end as a watery mush.

Queen Isabella of Spain boasted that she only took two baths in her whole life – one when she was born, and one before her wedding.

There are more bacteria in your mouth than there are people in the world.

Earwax comes in a range of colours including yellow, grey, brown and pumpkin orange.

An adult human contains enough water to fill three large buckets.

It would take 20 minutes to pour all the human urine produced in a single day over Niagara Falls.

If your head is chopped off, you can remain conscious for about 25 seconds!

If your fingers or toes get very cold, they can get frostbite. They slowly rot and turn black and have to be cut off to stop the rot spreading.

Electric signals from the brain can continue for 37 hours after death.

The women of the Karen tribe in Thailand traditionally wear masses of metal bands around their necks. The first bands are added on a girl's fifth birthday, and more are added every few months. If the bands are removed, the woman's weakened neck can't support her head. Removing the bands became an effective punishment.

While talking, we spit out 300 tiny drops of spit per minute.

In Scandinavian countries, people used to burn children's first teeth when they fell out in case witches found them and used them to cast an evil spell on the child.

The scabies mite burrows inside your skin, making long tunnels and causing horrible itching.

You sit on the largest muscles in your body! You have a *gluteus maximus* in each buttock.

By the time each of your red blood cells dies, it has travelled around the body some 250,000 times.

If you get pins and needles, it means you've squashed a nerve or two.

Joe Stalnaker from Arizona suffers from seizures. Luckily, he has a companion who can call an ambulance when it happens – his specially trained German shepherd dog, Buddy!

You have several different metals in your body, such as iron in your blood and potassium in your nervous system. Calcium is what you have the most of – that's what makes your bones and teeth hard.

A caterpillar has more muscles in its body that you do!

You have three sorts of rib: true ribs are attached to your spine and breastbone; false ribs are attached to your spine and lowest true ribs; floating ribs are attached to just the spine. No spare ribs, though…

There are no toilets on the moon, so astronauts have to wear a *maximum absorption garment* when they go on spacewalks. Yep, that's a big nappy!

People who exercise too much can develop athletic heart syndrome, where the heart becomes enlarged from having to pump extra blood around the body.

Your brain is a very demanding organ – it uses one-fifth of your body's blood, oxygen and energy supplies.

Joe Stalnaker from Arizona suffers from seizures. Luckily, he has a companion who can call an ambulance when it happens – his specially trained German shepherd dog, Buddy!

If a person's liver stops working, they will die within 24 hours.

Your heart is busy every second of the day – and it beats around 35 million times a year.

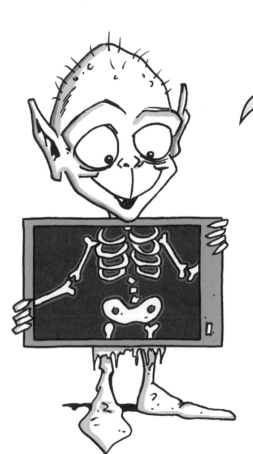

You have a tailbone at the end of your spine! It is called the *coccyx* – meaning 'cuckoo' – because it looks like a cuckoo's beak.

You can control some of your muscles, but others are doing their own thing! Your *involuntary muscles* control bodily functions such as heartbeat and digestion.

Sword-swallowers train themselves to control the gag reflex that occurs when something touches the soft palate at the back of the mouth. If you touch it, you'll vomit…so don't try it!

Your brain weighs half as much as your skin.

You have stripy muscles! Those joined to your bones – the skeletal muscles – are made up of light and dark coloured fibres that give a striped effect.

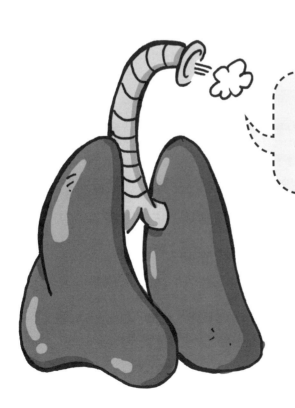

You will breathe in around 18 kilograms (40 pounds) of dust over your lifetime – that's about 18 large bags of flour!

One in 600 people are born with kidneys that are fused together in a horseshoe shape.

The brain cannot feel pain, so some brain surgery can be done while the patient is awake! The surgeon will then talk to the patient during the operation to make sure that healthy parts of the brain are not being affected.

Your body can manage for longer without food than it can without sleep.

When you feel thirsty, your body is already dehydrated. It's your brain's way of telling you to get a drink, quick!

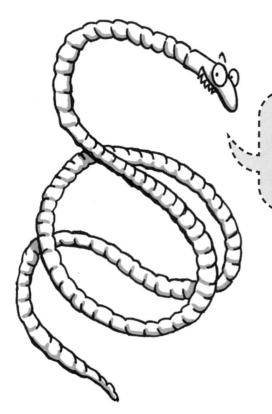

A broad tapeworm can grow in the intestine for decades, reaching a length of 10 metres/33 feet. Worst of all, you may not even know you have one...

Mosquitoes hate the smell of garlic, so you can try eating some to keep them at bay. You can ward off vampires into the bargain, too!

When South African woman Elsie van Tonder tried to help a seal back into the sea, it bit off her nose! A helpful bystander picked up her nose, but it couldn't be reattached.

There are more cases of heart attacks on a Monday than on any other day.

In severe cases of worms, a large group can clump together in a ball and cause a blockage in the intestine or bowel.

Amoebic dysentery is severe diarrhoea caused by a parasite that kills around 70,000 people every year. It can travel from the intestine to the liver, where it creates pus-filled abscesses.

Demodex mites are tiny parasites that live in eyebrows and eyelashes. They're very common, especially in older people. Under a microscope, they look like worms with stubby legs.

Mosquitoes spread malaria when they bite and pass on saliva containing parasites. The parasites then travel through the bloodstream and multiply in the liver and red blood cells.

You will breathe in around 18 kilograms (40 pounds) of dust over your lifetime – that's about 18 large bags of flour!

Body lice are even worse than head lice! They live in clothing and cause intense itching.

The female chigoe flea lays her eggs by burrowing into human skin headfirst, leaving her back end sticking out. Over two weeks, she feeds on blood and lays 100 or so eggs, before dying and falling out.

The lasting pain from an Arizona bark scorpion's sting feels like a series of electric shocks.

Despite being treated, some strains of malaria can recur years after the initial infection.

The Amazonian giant centipede delivers venom through its sharp claws, so if you come across one... don't touch!

You probably have two kidneys... but you could have more. People with extra kidneys don't find out until they have a scan for other problems. British teenager Laura Moon discovered she had four kidneys altogether when she had a scan for stomach pains!

Minute pirate bugs have a beak-like *proboscis* (a sucking mouthpart) that they stick into the skin. Ouch!

One of the largest human flea infestations in the UK was found on a farm where more than 130 million fleas carpeted the ground!

Pliny the Elder, an ancient Roman, said eating lion fat was a cure for epilepsy. If there were no lions around, sufferers could always try one of his other suggestions – dried camel's brain in vinegar!

Ancient Egyptian physicians used acacia thorns as needles when they stitched up wounds.

Bilharzia is a flatworm infection caught by paddling or swimming in tropical lakes. It can damage the stomach, bladder and liver, so think carefully next time you're tempted to go for a swim on holiday...

An ancient criminal punishment was to sew the condemned person inside a rotting animal skin and tie it to a tree. The criminal would then be eaten alive by the first hungry creature that came along.

Richard the Lionheart died from an arrow wound that became gangrenous.

Arctic explorer John Hornby tried to spend a year without food supplies by the Thelon River, in Canada, certain that he could live off the land. He starved to death after only a few months.

In World War I, soldiers used lumps of sphagnum moss as dressings for their wounds. It can soak up four times as much blood as cotton bandages.

French Admiral Gaspard de Coligny found a novel use for his bushy beard – he kept his toothpicks in it!

What gives faeces their normal colour is bilirubin, a brown substance that comes from the breakdown of old blood cells in the liver.

One medieval treatment for a skin infection was to rub cow dung on it.

Greek philosopher Aristotle believed that nose mucus came from the brain.

US trainee doctor Stubbins Firth was so convinced that *yellow fever* wasn't infectious that he drank a sufferer's 'fresh black vomit'. He escaped the deadly disease even though it is contagious (but transmitted through blood).

Your spine takes more strain when you laugh or cough than when you stand or walk. Some people have even developed back injuries from coughing.

Eighteenth-century toothpaste recipes included burnt bread and dragon's blood. It's not quite as gruesome as it sounds – dragon's blood was a red plant resin.

The dentures of US President George Washington were made from hippopotamus' teeth.

Neil Armstrong, the first man on the moon, was travel sick as a child.

It was against ancient Roman law to dissect human bodies; physicians of the time had to make do with dead pigs and monkeys for their research.

Medieval soldiers used a *trebuchet* to catapult things over castle walls at their enemies – including severed heads!

British Prime Minister William Gladstone lost his left forefinger in an accident while reloading a gun.

Greedy Swedish monarch King Adolf Frederick's biggest meal consisted of lobster, caviar, kippers and cabbage, followed by 14 servings of his favourite dessert. It was to be his last – he died shortly afterwards of digestion problems.

The terrifying 15th-century warrior Pier Gerlofs Donia was known for his ability to chop off several enemies' heads with one swing of his great sword.

An early *typhus* vaccine was made from squished body lice infected with the deadly disease!

Immediately after declaring on a TV show that he'd never felt better in his life, US author Jerome Irving Rodale died of a heart attack.

Pakistan is the home of dentistry – 9,000-year-old skeletons discovered there had drilled and capped teeth.

Jimmy Carter was the first American President to be born in a hospital.

People living in Pompeii were trapped under deep volcanic ash when Mount Vesuvius erupted in AD79. When the bodies decomposed, they left their shapes behind in the ash and plaster casts of them were made 2,000 years later.

The *influenza* pandemic of 1918 came to be known as 'Spanish flu', even though it started in America.

Obesity was frowned upon in ancient Rome. One account of the time tells of a large man having a breast reduction operation, as 'they looked unsightly and shameful'.

Franz 'The Flying Tailor' Reichelt designed a huge overcoat that doubled as a parachute. He demonstrated his invention in 1912 by jumping off the first deck of the Eiffel Tower, but it didn't work and he died in the fall.

The 17th-century Italian lady's poison of choice was Acqua Toffana: a lethal cocktail of arsenic, lead and belladonna (deadly nightshade). Perfect for using on an annoying husband!

The nail fungus *onychomycosis* can turn your nails green.

The back part of your brain deals with messages from your eyes, so badly bumping the back of your head can affect your sight.

Australian footballer Daniel Chick got so fed up with the painful injury to his left ring finger that he asked to have it amputated.

About 0.01 per cent of the population has internal organs on the opposite side to everyone else, with no ill effects – basketball player Randy Foye has *situs inversus* and is as fit as the next man!

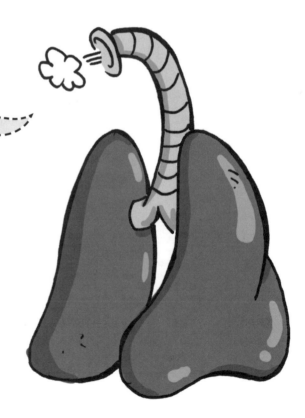

The painful eye infection *trachoma* is contagious and causes blindness, damaging the sight of around eight million people in the developing world.

When two-year-old Mackenzie Argaet had a liver transplant, there was one problem: the adult liver she received was too big. Her doctor used a novel idea to give it support and to stop it squashing vital blood vessels: he put in a ping pong ball!

Ever wondered why you salivate before throwing up? It's your body's way of protecting your teeth from the high acid levels in vomit.

If you could touch your brain, it would feel like jelly!

The rare phenomenon known as *Blaschko's lines* is characterized by pigmented stripes on a person's skin, particularly across the back.

More people are allergic to cows' milk than to any other food or drink.

Babies born with the rare condition *craniofacial duplication* have one head but two faces.

Your inner body regularly springs little leaks of blood, but the blood quickly clots to plug the hole. If it didn't clot, your insides would just keep bleeding!

A British man who was engulfed by clouds of mould when he opened compost in his garden suffered from acute *aspergillosis* – the spores invaded his lungs and damaged them so badly that he died.

In some developing countries, there is a custom of dressing a newborn baby's umbilical cord stump with animal dung to stop it bleeding. This often leads to infection and the serious illness *tetanus*.

Pig hearts are similar to ours, so pig heart valves are sometimes used in open-heart surgery to replace faulty human ones.

Your gallbladder is dark green... in case you were wondering!

Women who wear very high heels too often, suffer from pain in the ball of the foot. There are now Botox 'foot filler' injections available that give sufferers built-in foot pads... or they could just stop wearing ridiculous shoes!

Ever heard of *monkeypox*? It's similar to chickenpox; the difference is that you catch monkeypox from monkeys, but you catch chickenpox from... humans!

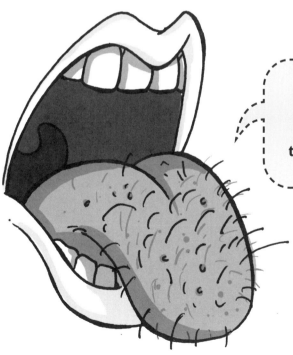

The fungal infection *black hairy tongue* causes the taste buds to swell and discolour, giving the tongue a dark, furry appearance.

The tropical virus *dengue fever* causes such bad joint and muscle pains that it is also known as 'bonecrusher disease'.

People with the rare condition *Naegeli Syndrome* have no fingerprints.

Lung pinprick condition is a rare hereditary illness in which microscopic holes appear in the lungs, making people breathe louder than usual.

All the food debris, mucous and dead cells on your tongue are a playground for the bacteria that cause bad breath smells when they multiply.

Soldiers in tropical climates can suffer from *jungle rot*, a fungal infection that begins with sores on the feet and spreads to the rest of the body.

A head injury or earwax build-up can cause *tinnitus* – a ringing, whistling or hissing noise in one or both ears... all the time!

In a rare birth defect known as *congenital cystic eye*, a baby is born with a fluid-filled cyst in place of an eye.

Sunburn damages your blood vessels so badly that it takes them months to repair themselves. It can also cause permanent damage, including skin cancer.

Conjunctivitis is a fairly common infection that makes the eyes red, itchy and gunky.
It's highly contagious, too…

If you could look inside your bones, you would see that they're full of holes – just like a sponge! If your bones were solid, they would be too heavy to move about.

There is no cure for the common cold, as there are hundreds of viruses that cause it.

American banjo player Eddie Adcock developed a hand tremor that affected his playing. To stop it, surgeons operated on his brain… while he was still awake and strumming on his banjo!

There is enough sulphur in a human body to kill all the fleas on a dog.

The energy from the food you need in one day is just enough to heat four teaspoons of water from freezing point to boiling.

Every minute, 30,000–40,000 skin cells drop off your body.

Godfrey Hill, from the UK, has 10 complete fingers and two thumbs, and has been accused of being an alien or the Messiah.

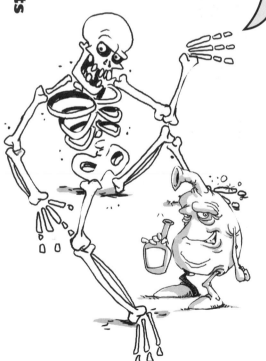

If you try to stop yourself from throwing up by closing your mouth, the vomit will just come out of your nose.

In the last minute, 300 million cells died in your body. Did you notice them go?

Horrible Food Facts

Napoleon's starving troops were told to eat the flesh of horses that had died on the battlefield. They used a sprinkling of gunpowder as seasoning!

A ripe jackfruit smells of rotten onions.

Entomophagy is the habit of eating insects – over 1,200 species of insects are gobbled down all over the world.

Animal fat from cooking meat is a common cause of sewer blockages. Thames Water flushers in central London once had to clear a solid lump of fat blocking 45 metres (150 feet) of sewer.

Two Scottish artists used their own blood to make black pudding (blood sausage). As if animal blood isn't disgusting enough?

Giblets are the heart, liver and gizzard (stomach) of a bird. You can eat them all if you want to!

African delicacy *mopani* worms are emperor moth caterpillars. They are prepared for frying by nipping off the ends and squeezing out the green guts… just like toothpaste from a tube!

Talcum powder is sometimes added to foods as an anti-sticking agent.

The French dish *oreilles de Christ* (Christ's ears) is made with pieces of deep-fried bacon fat. No ears in 'ere!

Cow's milk that has not been pasteurized can contain nasty bacteria, such as tuberculosis, salmonella, E. coli and diphtheria.

You can get Paralytic Shellfish Poisoning (PSP) from eating shellfish that have fed on toxic algae. Muscular and respiratory paralysis (which is death, basically) can occur within hours of digestion.

Butter and yogurt made from camel's milk are light green.

The edible white larvae of the New Zealand *Huhu* beetle can be up to 7 centimetres (3 inches) long. They taste like buttered chicken.

Livermush is a popular product in the southern United States, made from pig's liver, pig's head and cornmeal.

Brendan Brockbank won the World Pie-Eating Contest in Wigan, England, by wolfing down a humungous pie in just 37 seconds!

The *fatass ant* – guess what it looks like – has been a traditional Columbian food for hundreds of years and is often given as a wedding gift. Only the queen ants are edible and harvesting them is a painful business.

Used chewing gum was auctioned online in 2004. Pieces chomped by Britney Spears, Christina Aguilera, Eminem and Jessica Simpson were available to interested bidders.

Black moss or *hair moss* is a freshwater algae used in Chinese cooking. In its dried form, it looks like black human hair.

Apple pips contain a small amount of toxic cyanide, which causes vomiting, seizures and cardiac arrest. Don't panic if you swallow one – you'd need large amounts to be poisoned.

The Burnt Food Museum in Arlington, Massachusetts, showcases black, charred food. The museum had to close down temporarily... due to fire damage!

Tiny, fiery hot chillies used in Thai cooking are known as *phrik khii nuu,* which translates as 'mouse-dropping chillies'.

Charles Darwin was president of The Glutton Club at Cambridge University. He and his friends would meet to taste 'strange flesh', including hawk, bittern and owl.

Pocari Sweat is the name of a Japanese soft drink that is grey in colour. Mmmm, tempting!

The French cheese *Époisses de Bourgogne* is so stinky that it is banned from being taken on public transport in France.

Lead tastes sweet! Wine was sweetened with toxic lead sugar until the 17th century, giving those who drank it gradual lead poisoning.

British pensioner Margaret Haste keeps a hot cross bun as a reminder of her aunt, who died in 1899. The 108-year-old heirloom is kept wrapped in tissue inside a box.

British performance artist Mark McGowan turned himself into an English breakfast for two weeks in 2003. He sat in a bath of baked beans with two chips up his nose and 48 sausages strapped to his head.

Donkey meat was eaten in Britain until the 1930s.

US researchers ran trials on a drink containing pig whipworm eggs. They found that the hatched worms eased symptoms of bowel disorders in the people taking part.

Fancy a slice of pig's blood sausage, studded with chunks of pickled pig's tongue? Just ask for *Zungenwurst* next time you're in Germany!

Kumis is a Central Asian drink, made from horse's milk that is fermented in horse skin containers until slightly alcoholic.

Korean fermented soya bean paste (*doenjang*) smells of rotten fish.

The *fingered citron or Buddha's hand* is a giant citrus fruit so scary-looking that it has also been named *goblin fingers*. Mould can grow between the yellow 'fingers' but when fresh, the fragrant fruit is used for its zest.

Singaporean *pig's organ soup* is a mixture of pig intestine, stomach, blood cubes and pork slices. There are vegetables in it too, but you probably wouldn't notice those.

A young Wisconsin factory worker became trapped in a chocolate vat for two hours after he waded into it up to his waist to pull out the plug. Nearly death by chocolate!

Raw red kidney beans contain a toxic enzyme called *phytohaemagglutinin*, which causes severe vomiting and diarrhoea. The beans are made safe to eat by hours of soaking and boiling. Tinned ones are fine!

Anticuchos are South American goat heart or cow heart kebabs. A hearty meal on a stick.

A British chef was bitten by a highly venomous Brazilian wandering spider that had been hiding in bananas in his kitchen. He was quick-thinking enough to photograph the spider on his phone so that he could get the right treatment.

Fuqi feipian is a Chinese dish that translates as 'married couple's lung slices' and is made of thin slices of spiced cow's lung, served cold.

If you refrigerate bananas, you'll give them chill injury! As tropical fruits, they react badly to cold temperatures by going black and squishy.

Mad honey intoxication is caused by eating honey made from rhododendron nectar. Symptoms include vomiting, excessive salivating and sweating, and tingling around the mouth.

Eye protection is recommended for those sampling the maggot-ridden Sardinian delicacy *casu marzu* cheese. The larvae in it can jump as high as 15 centimetres (6 inches) when disturbed!

Filipino 'chocolate pudding' is in fact, a dark brown stew of pigs' organs in a spicy pigs' blood gravy.

The first bubble gum was developed in 1906 and was a failure. Called *Blibber-Blubber*, it had the consistency of children's modeling dough and produced sticky, wet bubbles.

The red food colouring carmine (€120) is made from crushed cochineal insects.

An outbreak of the disease *salmonella* in Britain during the summer of 2005 was traced to lettuces imported from drought-hit southern Spain. Desperate farmers had used their household sewage to water crops.

Dead insects go off quickly so should be eaten alive or immediately after being killed. Hopping insects need to be chilled or frozen before cooking so they don't jump out of the pan!

Japanese *basashi* vanilla ice cream is made with chunks of raw horseflesh. If you don't fancy that, there's always *yagi no aisu:* goat's milk and goat's meat ice cream.

Oiseaux sans têtes (headless birds) is a Belgian dish of sausage meat wrapped in veal slices.

Comedy actor Steve-O vomited after snorting super-hot Japanese *wasabi* in a stunt for *Jackass: The Movie.*

A bag of flour may be infested with tiny beetles called *weevils* that can spread the deadly E. Coli bacteria. They also like hiding in packets of cereal. You have been warned!

British woman Jo Carter ate 10.3 metres (34 feet) of raw stinging nettles to win the World Stinging Nettle-Eating Championship in 2006.

Rhubarb leaves contain a poison called *oxalic acid* that irritates the gut and causes kidney damage. Luckily, they taste pretty foul so it's unlikely anyone would eat enough to poison themselves.

Pickled turkey gizzard is a traditional dish in some parts of the midwestern United States.

Californian Olivia Chanes felt something metallic in the hot dog she was eating. An x-ray showed that she had swallowed a 9-millimetre (one-third-of-an-inch) bullet.

The strong smell of popular Chinese dish *stinky tofu* comes from it being fermented for as long as six months. It is sometimes black... even more appetizing!

British farmer Giles Peare is quite happy to snack on the slugs he finds on his farm. He thinks fried worms are tasty too.

11th-century Egyptians resorted to cannibalism when the Nile failed to flood for eight years in a row, causing a famine.

In the year 2000, food manufacturer Heinz produced tomato ketchups that were green, blue and purple. Everyone was quite happy with red, thank you, and the impostor sauces were discontinued.

Some traditional cheese-making procedures involve regular cleaning of the cheese's surface to rinse away the tiny cheese mites that feast on it.

In the Philippines, the eyes are considered the tastiest part of a steamed fish. Suck out the gloop and spit out the hard cornea.

British celebrity chef James Martin tried to make Brussels sprouts more appealing in 2004 by creating recipes for sprout ice cream, a sprout smoothie and a 'sproutini' cocktail.

Ever heard of a vegetable injury? The *cardoon* is a type of artichoke with a stalk that is covered in spines that can become lodged in the skin.

Severed heads, amputated limbs and internal organs went on display in a Thai bakery. The realistic-looking macabre items were made out of bread by art student Kittiwat Unarrom.

In traditional Italian cooking, a piece of sharpened horse's leg bone called a *spinto* is used to test whether a ham is cooked.

Cow's milk contains tiny amounts of pus and blood cells. If you're lucky, you might get some traces of antibiotics too.

The *death cap* is one of the world's most toxic mushrooms. Because it looks similar to edible mushrooms, it accounts for 50 per cent of all mushroom-poisoning cases. Symptoms include coma, jaundice and even death.

The edible part of a jackfruit is surrounded with sticky, white latex goo that clings to the fingers. Those in the know oil their hands before preparing one!

Japanese soldiers killed and ate eight American soldiers in 1945. They were later hanged for doing so.

Indian delicacy Bombay duck is, in fact, dried lizardfish. It's also known as *bummalo* and is so pongy that it has to be transported in airtight containers!

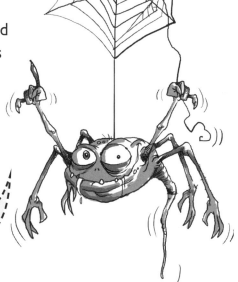

The Cambodian town of Skuon is known as Spiderville, famous for its dish of fried tarantula. The huge Thai zebra spiders are specially bred for food in holes in the ground.

Oranges imported into Europe from Israel in 1978 had been purposely contaminated with mercury by terrorists.

In 1951, the townspeople of French town Pont-Saint-Esprit were made ill by *pain maudit* (cursed bread) that made many of them psychotic. The grain used to make the flour was affected by *ergot*, a hallucinogenic fungus.

Popular British bar snack *pork scratchings* are bits of deep-fried pig skin… some with hair still attached.

Gelatine (also known as E441) is made by boiling up animal skin, cartilage and bone for hours on end. It is added to a range of foods such as gummy sweets and jelly.

New York Times journalist William Buehler Seabrook obtained a chunk of fresh human meat from a hospital so that he could cook and eat it for research. He said it tasted like veal.

Pets-de-nonne (nun's farts) are delicate Canadian cinnamon rolls. Nuns don't fart, surely?

Red whelks can sometimes be mistaken for edible whelks, but their saliva is highly toxic. If eaten, they will cause blurred vision and paralysis.

Around 50,000 horses are slaughtered each year in the US to be exported for meat.

Death Row prisoner Kenny Richey wrote his own cookbook based on his prison experiences. His *Death Row Recipes* book includes a fish toastie that is warmed up on a radiator.

At least 16,000 children die around the world each day from hunger-related causes.

British man Les Lailey celebrated his Golden Wedding anniversary with wife Beryl by opening... a 50-year-old can of chicken! The whole jellied chicken had been in their wedding day hamper.

Camel meat has been eaten in some parts of the world for centuries – the hump is apparently the best part.

Mould on decaying food can be white, green, brown, black, red or pink.

Police seized 30 tonnes (66,138 pounds) of rotten meat from a rat-infested London warehouse in 2003. The illegal meat that was allegedly destined for human consumption included decomposing lambs' brains, goat carcasses, gizzards and cows' feet.

The Papuan Korowai tribe practised cannibalism until around 1990.

Can you guess what honey ants taste like? For a tasty Australian bush tucker snack, just track down a nest, take an ant by the head and munch its sweet body.

Chakna is a spicy Indian stew made with goat stomach and a sprinkling of other tasty animal parts.

North-eastern Thai dish *yum khai mod daeng* is red ant egg salad. You can have extra ants if you ask nicely.

A 330-year-old cookery book found stored in a trunk in Derby, England, contained a section entitled 'A la mode ways of dressing the head of any beast'. It also gave recipes for marinated conger eel and hare mince pies.

Filipino fermented fish *bagoong terong* smells like raw sewage!

Chocolate is toxic to dogs, cats, horses and parrots, because their bodies cannot break down the chemical *theobromine* that comes from cocoa beans. If they eat too much, they can suffer from vomiting, diarrhoea and muscle spasms.

Toxic mushrooms such as the pure white *destroying angel* contain poison that destroys the liver and kidneys.

A British farmer added carrots to his cows' diet, but their milk turned pink! He solved the problem by importing white carrots from France.

Natural sausage casings are made from animal intestines.

The bacteria used for fermenting *Limburger* cheese are the same as the bacteria found on human skin that cause body odour. The monks who originally created the cheese used to pound it with their bare feet!

A family in Virginia opened their box of fried chicken to find a whole battered chicken's head inside!

A Florida jogger survived for four days on swamp water and leaves when he was trapped waist-deep in mud after taking a shortcut while out running.

Britain's first ever crocodile farm was set up in Cambridgeshire, England, where crocodiles are bred for food. The farmer helpfully says that the meat 'tastes like crocodile'.

The main ingredient in pepper spray is *capsaicin*, which comes from fiery chilli peppers. The spray causes tears, pain, coughing and temporary blindness.

Caffeine is a plant substance that paralyzes and kills insects. It is found in chocolate, cola, tea and coffee and is a central nervous system stimulant. Large amounts of caffeine can cause an irregular heartbeat, insomnia and muscle twitching.

65 million guinea pigs are eaten in Peru each year!

Beef tripe is from the first three of a cow's four stomachs: the *rumen* makes smooth tripe, the *reticulum* gives honeycomb tripe and book tripe comes from the *omasum*.

Elephant ears are a popular snack in the United States. Fortunately, they are not animal parts but pieces of fried dough sprinkled with sugar.

Shaw's Bistro and International Tapas Bar was the first restaurant in Scotland to serve rattlesnake, crickets and locusts.

An Edinburgh woman stopped eating her McDonald's cheeseburger when she noticed a huge spider in the box. When she looked inside the burger, there was another one in there too! The company issued an apology for the incident.

Asafoetida is a stinky spice that comes from plant sap and is also known as devil's dung or devil's dirt. It smells revolting as a powder but tastes delicious when cooked.

A traditional way to make African *amasi* (soured milk) was to leave unpasteurized milk out in the sun to fester for a couple of days!

Fried-brain sandwiches are a popular snack in some parts of the US.

Dark green-brown *grass jelly* is used in desserts and drinks in China and Southeast Asia. It really is jelly with grass in it.

Dozens of London residents were struck down by *diarrhetic shellfish poisoning* in 1998 after eating mussels from two of the capital's restaurants. It was the first case of the poisoning for 30 years.

Stinging nettles are a nutritious food and a little steaming gets rid of the sting. Nettle soup, anyone?

> A robber was pelted with chicken drumsticks by staff when he tried to hold up a fast-food restaurant at gunpoint in Sussex, England. He fled empty-handed.

Rennet is an enzyme taken from slaughtered calves' stomachs that is used in some traditionally-made cheeses to make them solid.

> Tests on 2000-year-old faeces discovered in Roman military toilets unearthed in Scotland, showed that the soldiers had enjoyed a meal made with eggs.

The Great Book of Horrible Facts

In medieval times, cow and deer innards were known as *umbles*. Umble pie was a popular dish among the lower classes and it's thought that this is where the phrase 'to eat humble pie' came from.

Large amounts of liquorice can cause liver damage. It can increase the amounts of the hormone *cortisol* in the liver, which raise blood pressure and blood sugar levels.

Swedish King Eric XIV was fatally poisoned by a bowl of arsenic-laced pea soup whilst in prison.

Sipunculid worm jelly is a delicacy in Xiamen, China. The marine worm burrows in sand and is known for its tentacled mouth.

A 2003 investigation by the British Coffee Association found that some coffees sold in Britain were contaminated with coffee bean mould, stones, twigs and 'floor sweepings'.

Devon colic was a type of lead poisoning suffered by people in Devon, England, after drinking the local cider in the 17th century. The cider presses were made of lead and lead shot was used to clean them.

Japanese fermented soya beans *nattou* come in a tacky goo that forms webby strings when pulled apart. They stink of blue cheese too!

Slátur is an Icelandic dish made by filling sheep stomachs with blood and fat.

The natural colour of margarine is grey, so yellow colouring is added to make it look more appetizing. It is illegal to sell margarine with colouring in Quebec.

Low quality cod liver oil smells of rotten fish and rancid oil. It tastes pretty yucky too!

Pokeweed leaves retain some of their poisonous toxins after being boiled. Despite this, poke salad remains a popular dish in the southern United States.

Black corn fungus, known as *huitlacoche*, is a delicacy in Mexico. The mould grows in damp corn after rain and makes the kernels swell up into big, deformed blobs.

The black stone in the *sapodilla* fruit has a hook at one end and can stick to the throat if swallowed.

Grilled chicken gizzards are a popular street food in many Southeast Asian countries.

Antarctic explorers Douglas Mawson and Xavier Mertz got severe vitamin A poisoning from eating husky liver after they lost their food supplies in a crevasse.

Lard is pig fat. Much of the lard sold in supermarkets is treated with bleaching and deodorising agents.

Tripas is a popular taco and burrito filling in Mexico. It's not tripe, but fried beef intestines.

Baltic herring is fermented for months to make a Swedish dish called *surströmming*. The fermentation process continues after canning, so the tin explodes on opening! It also releases a pungent liquid that surrounds the rotten fish.

Peanuts can be contaminated with a toxic mould called *aspergillus flavus*.

The thorny durian fruit from Southeast Asia has such a pungent odour (likened to stale vomit and rotten eggs) that it is banned from being taken into hotels and on public transport!

British man Brian Duffield can eat a whole raw onion in 1 minute 29 seconds.

After tasting his own '16 Million Reserve' super-hot chilli powder, Blair Lazar's tongue was swollen and painful for several days. His New Jersey company Extreme Foods makes fiery sauces with names like 'Mega Death'.

Jumiles are bitter-tasting stinkbugs that are used in Mexican sauces and taco fillings.

Boiled animal gunk *gelatine* is used by some synchronized swimmers to keep their hair in place as it does not dissolve in cold water.

'Green tripe' is usually brown or grey and refers to unwashed tripe. Tripe needs to be meticulously cleaned before you can eat it... if you really want to, that is.

The rennet used in the Brazilian cheese *queijo coalho* comes from guinea pig stomach linings.

Anisakis is a worm that lives in fish. It is destroyed by extreme temperatures but a person who eats raw, salted or pickled fish that is infected will contract *anisakiasis*: severe stomach pain and vomiting will follow and larvae may be coughed up.

Hog maw is a Pennsylvanian German dish of pig's stomach stuffed with sausage and potatoes, traditionally eaten on New Year's Day.

Mexican delicacy *chapulines* are fried grasshoppers. The grasshoppers must be thoroughly cooked as they often carry worms that can also infest humans.

Menudo and *mondongo* are South American stews made with slow-cooked diced tripe, sometimes with trotters added. Nicaraguan folklore says the stew has healing powers.

Microbial rennet is used in cheesemaking as an alternative to animal rennet and is made from fermented mould. Mmm, much tastier.

An Ohio woman felt something gristly in her mouthful of salad at a restaurant and was horrified to discover that it was a human fingertip, complete with nail! The chef had sliced it off whilst chopping the salad and had rushed off to hospital without it.

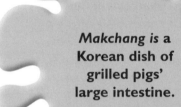

Makchang is a Korean dish of grilled pigs' large intestine.

Popular South American soft drink *Inca Kola* looks like urine and tastes like bubble gum.

Yellow food colourings *tartrazine* and *Sunset Yellow FCF* are derived from coal tar, which is the sludge left over when coal is made into coke. Both are banned in Norway but widely used elsewhere.

Shkembe chorba is a Bulgarian soup made with beef tripe and milk.

Flavours of ice cream available in Japan include octopus, ox tongue, cactus, chicken wing and crab.

The Roman emperor Nero kept a 'glutton' – an Egyptian slave who ate everything he was given to eat, including human flesh.

To make especially tender beef, the Japanese shut cattle in the dark, feed them beer and employ special cattle masseurs to massage them by hand three times a day.

Stink heads are a traditional Alaskan dish. Fish heads – often from salmon – are buried in pits lined with moss for a few weeks or months until rotten. They are then kneaded like pastry to mix up all the parts and eaten.

Argentinian gauchos keep a piece of beef under their saddles so that it's pummelled until tender as they ride around all day. It's said that the dish steak tartar came from Mongolian warriors doing the same and then eating the steak raw.

The Spanish eat the traditional rural cheese *cabrales* when it is 'con gusano' – crawling with live maggots.

In India, ants are roasted, ground to a paste and served as chutney.

A stew eaten at a funeral in Stone Age Wales was made from shellfish, eels, mice, frogs, toads, shrews and snakes.

In Sardinia, cheese is left in the sun for flies to lay their eggs in. When the maggots hatch, the swarming mass is spread on bread and eaten.

An 18th-century recipe for making an enormous egg suggests sewing 20 egg yolks into an animal bladder, then dropping it into another animal bladder filled with 20 egg whites and boiling it all together.

In 1919, a tidal wave of treacle swept through Boston, USA. A storage tank burst, spilling 7.5 million litres (2 million gallons) of it into the streets. It poured over houses, knocking them down, in a wave two storeys high.

During the Second World War, people in the UK were urged by the government to make the most of wild foods, and were given recipes for cooking roast squirrel, rook casserole, stewed starlings and baked sparrows.

Odd crisp and potato chip flavours available around the world include octopus, seaweed, banana, and sour cream and squid.

The Insect Club, a restaurant in the USA, serves only dishes made with insects. The menu includes cricket pizza, insect chocolates and 'insects in a blanket' – crickets, mealworms and blue cheese in puff pastry.

In 1971, a man found the head of a mouse in a bar of chocolate.

Condemned prisoners are traditionally allowed a delicious last meal. In some US states, it's not actually their last meal, but is served a day or two before the execution and is called a 'special meal'.

Tradition tells that the French cheese Roquefort was discovered when a shepherd abandoned his lunch in a cave to chase a pretty girl he saw outside. When he came back months later, the cheese had gone mouldy but still tasted good.

Durian is a fruit the size of a football, covered in spikes, that smells like rotting meat. It's supposed to taste good, though!

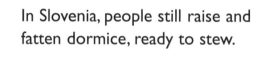

Roman banquets often featured hummingbirds cooked in walnut shells and roasted stuffed dormice, sometimes rolled in honey and poppy seeds. The Romans even had farms producing dormice because they were so popular.

In Slovenia, people still raise and fatten dormice, ready to stew.

In Nepal, Tibet and parts of China, black tea is served with yak butter, made from the milk of the yak.

During the First World War, Germany suffered such food shortages that people ate dogs and horses, and even the kangaroos from the zoos!

Raake orret is eaten in Norway. Trout caught in a freshwater stream are stored in salted water with a little sugar and kept in a cool place, such as the garage, for months before eating.

P'tcha is an Eastern European Jewish food made by stewing calves' feet until they turn to jelly.

Ambuyat, eaten in Brunei, is made from pulp from the sago palm, stewed in water for several hours. The same mixture is made to stick the roof on a house!

Also in Brunei, the sago worm which lives inside rotting sago palms is often cooked and eaten.

In Northern Australia, children often eat green ants. Pick them up, squish the head so they don't nibble you, and bite off the body.

In Madagascar, people make a stew from tomatoes and zebras.

Pruno is a 'wine' made by American prisoners from a mixture of fruit, sugar cubes, water and tomato ketchup left to fester in a bin bag for a week. In some prisons, pruno causes so many discipline problems that fruit has been banned.

In the Japanese countryside, salamanders and skinks are grilled on sticks and served with lettuce.

A restaurant in Osaka, Japan, serves whale ice cream made from the blubber of the minke whale.

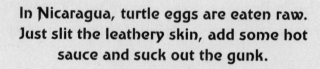

In Nicaragua, turtle eggs are eaten raw. Just slit the leathery skin, add some hot sauce and suck out the gunk.

Cinemas in Colombia serve paper cones filled with giant fried or toasted ants.

A rat restaurant in China sells rat and snake soup, rat kebabs, steamed rat with rice and crispy fried rat.

In Newfoundland, Canada, seal flipper pie is a traditional dish for the end of a seal hunt.

A restaurant in Changsha, China, offers food cooked in human breast milk.

Think cabbage is horrid? In Korea, it is sometimes buried in clay pots with salt for many months before it's eaten – this dish is called *kimchi,* and is served with most meals.

Alligator kebabs are popular in southern Louisiana, USA.

In Fiji, people starve a pig for a week, then feed it veal when it is very hungry. A few hours later, they kill the pig and remove the half-digested veal, which they cook and eat.

In Texas, there's an annual rattlesnake roundup. What to do with all the rattlesnakes? Skin them, gut them, cut them into chunks, cover them in batter and deep fry them.

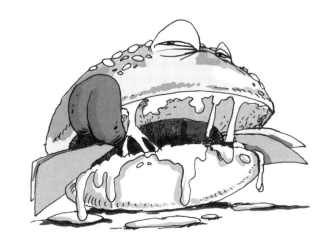

Another way of cooking snake in Texas – cut the head off, skin and gut it, poke a stick into the neck, wrap the snake loosely around the stick and roast over a campfire.

Iguanas are a popular and free food in Central America – they can often be caught in backyards.

In China, people eat jellied ducks' blood.

Slimy green stuff that looks like mucus is supposedly the best part of a lobster or crayfish. It's found in the head. Some Americans eat the main part of the lobster meat and then suck the head to get the gunge out.

As early as the ninth century, the Basques of Spain hunted whales, and whale tongue was considered a great delicacy.

Oellebroed is a Danish soup made from stale rye bread soaked in water, then boiled with beer and sugar and served with cream. It's possible to buy instant oellebroed powder – just add water.

Cibreo is an Italian dish that consists of the cooked combs from roosters.

Spam is a luncheon meat used as a filling for sandwiches. At a Spam-cooking contest, one contestant made Spam-chip cookies!

In Canada, deep-fried cod tongues are a popular dish.

The street markets of Indonesia sell whole, smoked bats.

McDonald's in Hong Kong sells a sweetcorn pie in a sweet pie crust, the same as apple pies in the West.

An international contest to find the best recipe for cooking earthworms included entries of stews, salads and soups but was won by a recipe for applesauce surprise cake. Guess what the surprise was…

Baby mouse wine, from China, is a bottle of wine packed with baby mice, to add flavour.

Jack Fuller was buried in a pyramid in Sussex, England, in 1811. It's said by local people that inside it, he is seated at a table with a roast chicken and a bottle of port.

Some Arctic explorers have been poisoned by eating polar bear liver. The polar bear eats so much fish that fatal levels of Vitamin D collect in its liver.

A restaurant in Pennsylvania, USA, offers a hamburger that weighs 4 kilograms (9 pounds). No one has yet managed to finish one.

The Chinese make a soup from the swim bladder of fish. It's the spongy organ that helps fish to stay at the right depth and upright in the water.

Drunken shrimps, served in China, are live shrimps swimming in a bowl of rice wine. The idea is to catch them with chopsticks and bite the heads off.

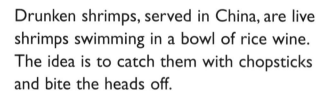

Bedouin people cook a camel's hump by burying it underground and lighting a fire over the top of it. When they dig it up and eat it, the top is cooked, but the bottom is still mostly raw and bloody.

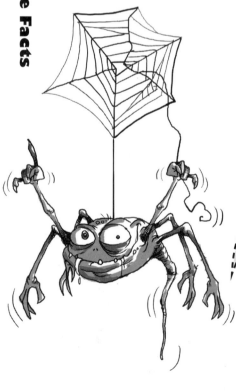

In Ness, Scotland, people kill young gannets – a type of seabird – to eat. The claws are the most highly prized part.

Eskimos have been known to make seagull wine – put a seagull in a bottle of water, wait for it to go off and drink!

Crispy fried duck or chicken feet are a delicacy in China. In the USA, whole chicken feet are sometimes pickled or made into soup.

Around 50 tonnes of food will pass through your stomach over your lifetime.

In the Philippines, the eyes are considered the tastiest part of a steamed fish. Suck out the gloop and spit out the hard cornea.

Fried chicken cartilage is served as a bar snack in Japan.

Marmite, a favourite English spread for toast, is made with the leftover yeasty sludge from brewing beer.

Snake wine in China is a very potent alcoholic drink, spiced with juice from the gall bladder of a live snake.

In Wales, rook pie was considered a tasty way to get rid of a bird that might otherwise eat the crops.

Nutrias are large rodents that live some of the time in the water. They are a pest in Louisiana, where local authorities are encouraging people to eat them – with little success, as they don't taste too good.

A traditional dish in London is eels boiled and served cold in jelly.

In the southern USA, squirrel brains are cooked while still in the head. You then crack the skull and scoop the brains out with fingers and fork.

In Hungary, scrambled eggs are fried up with the blood from a freshly slaughtered pig.

Some prisoners have big appetites. Richard Beavers, executed in Texas in 1994, ate for his last meal: 6 pieces of French toast with butter and syrup, 6 barbecued spare ribs, 6 pieces of bacon (burnt), 4 scrambled eggs, 5 sausage patties, French fries with ketchup, 3 slices of cheese, 2 pieces of yellow cake with chocolate fudge icing, and drank 4 cartons of milk.

Biltong is favoured as a snack by rugby supporters in South Africa. It's dried strips of any meat – elephant, eland, antelope…

In Indonesia, deep-fried monkey toes are eaten by sucking the meat straight off the bone.

In Sweden, people make dumplings from flour, reindeer blood and salt.

In Japan, the blowfish is a delicacy, even though it contains a poison gland which, if not properly removed, kills anyone who eats it.

An omelette costing $1000 (about £600) and called the Zillion Dollar Lobster Frittata was sold by a restaurant in New York. It contains a whole lobster and 280 grams (10 ounces) of caviar, as well as eggs, cream, potatoes and whisky.

In Georgia, there is a price limit of $20 (about £12) on the last meal a prisoner can order.

Small songbirds cooked and eaten whole have been so popular in Italy that many types have been wiped out completely.

In Sweden and Norway, roast reindeer is a national dish.

Many cheap meat products such as sausages and burgers are made from 'mechanically recovered meat' which consists of a meat slurry collected from washing bones and mincing up parts of the dead animal that aren't used for anything else.

In the Philippines, chicken heads may be made into stew or barbecued whole.

Jellyfish can be dried, salted and eaten. In the Gilbert Islands, in the western Pacific Ocean, jellyfish ovaries are served fried.

Aztecs gave people who were to be human sacrifices many last meals – they fattened them up for up to a year.

The Russian Jewish dish *kishke* is made by stuffing a chicken skin with flour, butter and spices and boiling it in chicken stock. Dry it out, then cut it into slices as a snack.

In China and Japan, sheets of dried jellyfish are sold for soaking and turning back into slimy jellyfish ready for cooking.

The ancient Greeks, Egyptians and Romans all gave condemned prisoners a last meal.

The Chinese eat monster barnacles the size of an adult's fist.

The town of Bunol, in Spain, has an annual tomato fight when up to 25,000 people throw around 100 tonnes (220,000 pounds) of tomatoes at each other. The streets can be flooded up to 30 centimetres (12 inches) deep with juice.

It takes around seven seconds for a piece of food to reach your stomach after you have swallowed it.

In the Samoan Islands, the intestines of sea cucumbers are sold in jars, steeped in seawater. The sea cucumber is a slithery, tube-like animal and not a cucumber at all. When it's cooked, it's called a sea slug.

The alcoholic drink *mescal* has a cactus maggot preserved in the bottle.

In the UK, game – wild animals and birds shot in the fields – is often hung until it is 'high', which means it is hung up on a hook until it starts to go off.

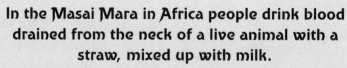

In the Masai Mara in Africa people drink blood drained from the neck of a live animal with a straw, mixed up with milk.

Raw, pickled jellyfish are eaten in the Samoan Islands.

Yeast are tiny fungi (mould), present in bread, beer and wine. The yeast eat sugar in the ingredients, making the gas which forms the bubbles in beer and wine and the holes in bread.

Eels are sold live in markets around the world and killed just before cooking – or before putting in the bag to go home, if you don't want the bag wriggling all the way.

Orangutan lips used to be a delicacy in Vietnam.

The British black pudding is a sausage made of congealed pigs' blood with lumps of fat embedded in it. It is often fried and eaten for breakfast.

Soft ice cream of the type sold in ice cream vans is given its slithery smoothness by an extract of seaweed.

Baby eels, called elvers, are eaten in parts of Europe, including east England. They are very thin, so lots are cooked, tangled together like spaghetti.

In France, calves' eyes are soaked in water, then boiled and stuffed and finally deep fried in breadcrumbs.

Most US states don't allow alcohol or tobacco at a prisoner's last meal.

Cow's tongue is often sold with the salivary glands – the parts that make spit – ready for boiling. The tongue can weigh up to 2.3 kilograms (5 pounds).

Although your gastric juices contain powerful acids, they cannot digest chewing gum. Small amounts will get through the digestive system, but too much can cause a serious blockage… so always spit it out.

To make the expensive *pâté de foie gras*, geese are forcibly fattened with grain so that their liver swells to many times its natural size.

In Mexico, the alcoholic drink tequila is often served with a worm in the glass – the worm should be swallowed whole with the drink.

In England, lampreys – a fierce fish that looks like an eel – are traditionally cooked in a sauce flavoured with their own blood.

Romany people in Europe, and poor peasants, used to cook wild hedgehogs by rolling them in mud and baking them in the embers of a fire. When the mud dries, the spines can be peeled off with the mud.

Roast dog is sold on the streets of Vietnam. The back half of the dog comes with the tail intact.

The eggs of the sturgeon fish are called *caviar*, and are so valuable that an operation is sometimes used to remove them without harming the fish, which then goes on to make more eggs. Previously, the fish was gutted while still alive so that the eggs could be as fresh as possible.

In Central and South America, iguana meat is highly prized.

The French *cervela* sausage is made with the brains of pigs.

Mealworms – golden-coloured larvae that eat grain – are farmed in the USA and sold live in pots of bran for cooking. The bran is for the mealworms to eat while they are waiting, as otherwise they will eat each other.

Sheep's eyeballs are eaten in some Arab countries of North Africa.

In China, bear paws are roasted in clay – the fur comes off with the dried clay when they are done.

In France, rats found in wine cellars were sometimes cooked in a sauce flavoured with red wine, over a fire of burning wine barrels.

The Aztec dish *tlacatalalli* was a stew made from corn and human beings.

In the 1800s, naturalist Frank Buckland served meals such as mice on toast, roasted parrots and stewed sea slug. He tried to make soup from an elephant's trunk, but even after several days' cooking it was still too chewy.

Bird's nest soup is a delicacy in China. It's made from the nests of a special variety of swift that builds its nest from dried strands of its own spit. The nest is soaked in water to soften it, then any sticks and feathers are removed before it is made into a gluey, sticky soup.

Truffles are a kind of fungus that grow underground in forests in Europe. Truffle hunters use pigs to smell them out. The best truffles are extremely valuable.

In the Middle Ages, a peacock was often roasted with its feathers on. The skin was inflated first to stop the feathers burning, and then pierced when the bird was cooked so that it appeared as though it were alive when served.

Some Amazonian tribes used to make a soup with the ground bones of their dead relatives.

At one Roman banquet, a slave stabbed the stomach of a roast boar to release a flock of live thrushes.

In Texas, armadillos are sometimes roasted in their shells, stuffed with carrots, apples and potatoes.

The Akoa pygmy tribe eat elephant meat with a serving of live maggots.

In some countries where people don't have food processors or forks, mothers chew up food to put into their babies' mouths.

Some Jewish people eat the braised udder of a cow.

Worms steamed whole in a jelly are a tasty treat in China.

The oldest surviving piece of chewing gum is 9,000 years old.

In Vietnam, cobra hearts are a common snack. They can be eaten raw, even still beating, with a small glass of cobra blood or dropped into a glass of rice wine. The kidney is often included as an extra tidbit.

US Air Force pilot, Captain Scott O'Grady, was shot down over Bosnia in 1995 and survived for six days eating only ants.

In 1135, King Henry I of England died from eating too many lampreys – a kind of eel that sucks its victims to death.

The skin of dead eels is so hard to remove that some people pull it off with pliers.

Camels' feet are cooked in a light stock and served with vinaigrette. Only the feet of young camels are considered tasty.

Camel feet can also be cooked in camel milk.

The original recipe for baked beans included bear fat and maple syrup.

The Scottish dish haggis is made by cutting up the heart, lungs, liver and small intestine of a calf or sheep and cooking it with suet, oatmeal, onions and herbs inside the animal's stomach.

Australian aborigines like to eat witchetty grubs – the larvae of the ghost moth – raw and wriggling. Or they can be barbecued on a skewer for a couple of minutes, like a kebab.

A restaurant in England recently offered snail porridge on its menu.

In the Faroe Islands, a favourite dish is puffin stuffed with rhubarb.

In China, eggs are buried underground until they go exceptionally bad and are then sold and eaten as 'hundred-year-old' eggs. In fact, they are about two years old. The yolks turn green and the whites turn grey or black.

In China, shark fin soup is made from the salted, sun-dried fins of sharks. It is like a bowl of glue, as the fin contains a lot of gelatine.

People in ancient China ate mice as a delicacy.

Roman feasts sometimes included the popular delicacy flamingo tongues.

For his last meal, murderer Victor Feguer chose a single olive.

Some Amazonian people eat omelettes made from tarantula eggs.

Honey found in ancient Egyptian tombs has been tasted by archaeologists and found to be edible still, after thousands of years.

If you eat too many carrots, you will turn orange.

Fried crickets have been a favourite food in China for centuries.

The Japanese make *natto* by leaving soy beans to rot in straw until slimy and sticky – and very smelly.

The *Air Force Survival Manual* issued to US airmen explains which bugs to eat in an emergency for maximum taste and nutrition.

The last meal of Oklahoma City Bomber Timothy McVeigh was almost a litre (2 pints) of mint chocolate-chip ice cream.

Australian supermarkets sell tins of witchetty grub soup.

In France, over 40,000 metric tons (88 million pounds) of snails are consumed every year.

Mealworms are supposed to taste better if cooked while still alive.

Sea slug is eaten in China and Spain. It's often sold dried and has to be soaked to restore it to its slimy, squishy glory.

Blood soup is popular in many parts of the world. In Poland, people eat a duck blood soup called *czarnina*; in Korea, pig blood curd soup is called *seonjiguk*; and in the Philippines people eat a pig blood stew called *dinuguan*.

Iowa State University's Department of Entomology has published recipes for cooking with insects, including banana worm bread, crackers and cheese dip with candied crickets and mealworm fried rice.

Sun-dried maggots have been eaten across the world, from China to North America.

In Ghana, half of the locally produced meat comes from rats.

Central American wedding feasts often included honeyed ants.

When a pig is roasted in Cuba, the skull is cracked open and each guest takes a spoon to share scoops of brain.

In 1973, a Swedish sweets salesman was buried in a coffin made of chocolate.

In Mexico, a black fungus which infects maize is canned and sold. It looks like black slime with a few yellow lumps.

Oriental cockroaches, also known as water bugs, are roasted and eaten in China – just leave the wings and legs.

The Korean delicacy *sannakji* consists of still-wriggling slices of octopus tentacle.

In the Philippines, fertilized duck or chicken eggs are cooked and eaten – with the unhatched chick partly grown inside. It's called *balut*, in case you want to avoid it on the menu.

Oysters are always eaten raw – alive – in the UK and USA.

In Cambodia, giant grilled spiders are a popular street snack.

An American delicacy called headcheese, similar to British brawn, is made by cooking a whole cow or pig head into a mush and letting it cool into a jelly-like mass.

In China, people get their own back on poisonous scorpions by frying them. They are said to taste rather like cashew nuts.

Native Alaskan Indians bury salmon eggs in a jar for 90 days and eat them when they are truly rotten.

Until 1999, it was legal to enjoy ortolan in France – a tiny, rare, song bird, fattened in a dark box to three times it normal size then drowned in brandy and spit roasted for a few minutes before being eaten whole, innards included. (It was okay to leave the head and beak.) Traditionally, it was eaten with a napkin draped over your head and the plate so that none of the delicious smell could escape.

In Finland, people cook blood pancakes.

Kakambian, from the Philippines, is made of diced goat – skin, hair, fat and meat all mixed together.

Delicacies enjoyed in Iceland include puffin and *svie* – singed and boiled sheep's head.

In some parts of Asia, monkey brains are a delicacy – but it's a myth that they are eaten from the head while the monkey is still alive.

In Mongolia, camel or horse milk is stored in a cleaned horse stomach or hide bag and hung up in the *ger* (tent). Everyone who passes the door has to stir or hit the bag. It slowly ferments into a slightly alcoholic, cheesy, yoghurt drink which everyone drinks, even children.

At the winter festival of Thorrablot, Icelanders eat *hákarl* – rotten shark. Shark meat is buried in the ground for six to eight weeks then dried in the open air for two months.

Bagoong is a very smelly, fermented paste made from mashed shrimps and eaten in the Philippines.

On the Pacific island of Palau, whole fruit bats, complete with skin, may be ordered in restaurants as a starter or main course.

In southern Africa, large caterpillars called *mopani* can be bought in tins.

Morcilla is a Puerto Rican sausage made with rice boiled in pigs' blood, stuffed into a sausage skin and then fried.

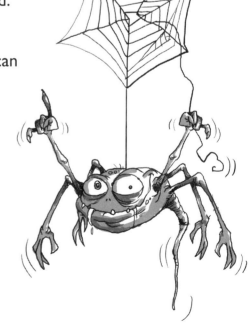

In Ecuador, a family barbecue can include guinea pig and snake kebabs.

In North Africa, people eat fried termites.

In Brazil, people eat barbecued armadillo.

In Hubei Province, China, eels are served whole. The correct way to eat one is to bite through just behind the head and pull out the insides with chopsticks.

In Hong Kong, you can buy packets of crispy fried crabs like packets of crisps.

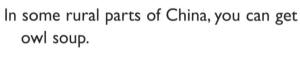

The Japanese dish *shiokara* is made by fermenting squid in old fish guts.

Rocky Mountain oysters, or prairie oysters, are calves' testicles – enjoyed fried in parts of the USA.

In some rural parts of China, you can get owl soup.

In Korea, it's possible to buy canned silkworm pupae, or bags of silkworms, from street vendors. The idea is to crunch the end off the grub and suck out the juices.

Spider wine, from Cambodia, is actually rice wine – the spiders are added later.

Horrible
Animal Facts

The fearsome coconut crab can crack coconuts with its mighty pincers. The land crab is also nicknamed the 'robber crab', as it has been known to steal shiny objects from houses and tents.

A dung beetle can move a ball of manure that is hundreds of times heavier than its own weight.

A hippopotamus will spin its tail while defecating to mark as much territory as possible with its faeces.

Blister beetles secrete a poison that leaves a painful blister on the skin.

A woman tried on a pair of jeans in an Okinawa shop, only to be stung in the leg by a scorpion that was hiding inside them! Although the sting was not fatal, the woman was hospitalized for several days.

The star-nosed mole in North America looks like its nose just exploded! It has 22 wriggly pink tentacles on the end of its snout, which it uses to detect and identify prey in a matter of milliseconds.

Only female midges bite you and will slurp up your blood for up to four minutes.

Forty kamikaze birds crashed into windows and broke their necks in Vienna after becoming drunk on fermented berries.

The fangs of the Australasian funnel-web spider are so sharp that they have been known to penetrate fingernails and soft shoes.

Some cockroaches can run at over 5 kilometres (3 miles) per hour, travelling 50 times their body length each second. If you could do that, you could run faster than a racing car!

A *zoonosis* is any infectious disease that can be transferred between animals and people.

A bear shot by a hunter in Canada in 2006 was found to be a grizzly-polar bear hybrid, the first ever documented. Suggested names in the media for the unusual bear have been a 'pizzly' or a 'grolar bear'. The hunter kept the bear's carcass as a trophy.

Some birds swallow stones or grit to help break up the food in their stomachs and then regurgitate them later.

A pond in Hamburg was dubbed the 'pond of death' after hundreds of its toads mysteriously exploded, scattering entrails more than 3 metres (10 feet) away.

The *slow worm* is a legless lizard that can shed its tail if attacked.

Authorities in Iowa investigating complaints by neighbours discovered that a house contained 350 snakes and 500 assorted rodents. Only six illegal snakes were removed, as the animals were well looked-after.

Animal manure produces heat as it decomposes. It has been known for large piles of manure to burst into flames.

Baboons have rough, nerveless callouses on their bottoms so that they can sit anywhere in comfort!

The rattle on a rattlesnake's tail is made of rings of dead skin. It builds up as the snake grows older, so the louder the rattle the larger the snake.

Vixens let out a long, eerie wail that sounds like a crying baby during the breeding season.

There are 18 different kinds of piranha fish, but only four of them are dangerous.

A golden retriever in California gave birth to a puppy with green fur. Its owner named the puppy Wasabi, which is a green Japanese condiment made with horseradish.

If agitated, the fierce *Tasmanian devil* (the world's largest carnivorous marsupial) releases a foul odour.

A pinecone shortage in eastern Russia drove a gang of ravenous squirrels to attack and eat a stray dog.

Hollywood kangaroo Feznik had plastic surgery to reconstruct his lip after he was attacked by a wolf.

A 'sausage fly' is actually a male driver ant with a bloated, sausage-shaped abdomen.

Some fish in Antarctica have white blood! This is because their blood has very low levels of the chemical that makes blood red (*haemoglobin*) and contains natural antifreeze to stop them freezing in the icy waters.

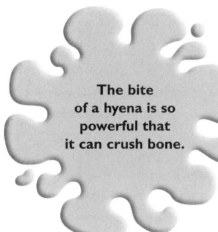

The bite of a hyena is so powerful that it can crush bone.

A naturist in Australia received burns to 18 per cent of his body when he poured petrol down a hole and set fire to it in an attempt to get rid of a deadly funnel-web spider.

Pigs do not sweat. They roll about in mud to keep cool in hot weather!

Birds do not urinate. Their urine and faeces are all mixed together to make one sloppy dropping.

Lurking beneath the cute-looking fluffy *puss caterpillar*'s soft hairs are poisonous spines. When touched, the spines break off and get lodged in the skin, causing intense pain, numbness, blisters and a rash.

A Kenyan elephant that slipped into a septic tank whilst trying to eat bananas on a farm was then killed and eaten by villagers.

Horses often chew at fly eggs and maggots on their legs and end up swallowing them, so they get a stomach full of crawling maggots.

The *wheel bug* has a cog shape on its back and its bite causes agonizing pain that can last for up to six hours.

Dogs love a bit of fresh tripe, even if the cow's stomach still has the remains of the cow's last meal stuck to it.

The eyes of the golden mole are covered with skin and fur. The mole lives in the desert and only comes out at night, so it has no need for eyes anyway. It looks like a golden hairball with legs!

Camels have three eyelids. They need them as protection against sun and sand.

The male duck-billed platypus has a sharp poisonous spur on its hind foot that can inflict severe pain on humans.

Scotsman David Evans was sentenced to six months' imprisonment for using a wet fish as an offensive weapon. He had slapped a passer-by round the face with it.

Green muscardine disease is a fungus that kills insects. The spores enter the insect and grow inside it, eventually covering the insect's outer body with green mould.

Many fly maggots eat dead flesh, but those of the screw-worm fly eat healthy flesh. If they infest an animal or human wound, they burrow in and destroy the healthy tissue around it, making the wound far worse.

A man was fined 25,000 Australian dollars (about £15,000) after hiding six rare birds' eggs in his underwear and trying to smuggle them out of Sydney airport.

A German shepherd dog was successfully trained to sniff out sheep droppings that were infected with worms on an Australian sheep farm.

A hyena can chew a broken bottle without hurting itself.

British sunbather Sally Brown was almost killed when a calf fell from the cliff-side field 15 metres (50 feet) above and landed on the beach beside her.

Locust swarms cause traffic accidents in hot countries when cars skid on all the squashed ones!

The Saharan desert ant can survive in temperatures of over 50 degrees Celsius (122 degrees Fahrenheit) and feeds on other insects that have frazzled in the heat.

A kangaroo can disembowel an attacking dog with its hind legs as it grips the dog with its forepaws.

A woman found a plastic lunch box in an Edinburgh street and opened it to find it was full of baby boa constrictors. Snake sandwich, anyone?

A pair of pigs in northern Italy became so enormous that they could not be moved and had to be slaughtered and taken from their sty in pieces. The pigs weighed 200 kilograms (440 pounds) each.

Fire ants are so called because a bite from one feels like a nasty burn on your skin.

British artist Damien Hirst pickled a shark measuring 4.3 metres (14 feet) in more than 900 litres (200 gallons) of formaldehyde. He called his work *The Physical Impossibility of Death in the Mind of Someone Living*.

Eastern European peasants used to make wound dressings out of spiders' webs. In fact, spider silk has antiseptic properties, so it wasn't such a bad idea.

Lizardfish have sharp teeth on their tongues. Ouch!

Click beetles are so called because they leap high into the air with a loud 'click' sound. Some of them glow in the dark, too.

Royal Bengal tigers have the longest canine teeth of all big cats, measuring an average of 10 centimetres (4 inches). The tigers frequently attack and eat people in the Sundarbans region of India and Bangladesh.

Cow dung sets hard in hot, dry countries and also contains a natural mosquito repellent, so is sometimes used to line rustic floors and walls. Caked cow dung is also used as a fuel when cooking.

The olive baboon has olive green skin.

The female golden silk orb-weaver spider is at least five times bigger than the male. She's definitely the boss!

US researchers discovered that *cottonmouth snake* venom was extremely effective at removing blood stains from white clothes.

Chinese genetic scientists have developed pigs that glow in the dark. The spooky porkers were created using injections of fluorescent green protein into the pig embryos.

Christmas Island is plagued with yellow crazy ants. These are aggressive ants that nest anywhere, form supercolonies with several queens and eat anything that moves, including birds, reptiles and even crabs!

The Peruvian booby bird uses its own droppings to make its nest.

Stargazer fish have two large poisonous spines on their backs and can also deliver electric shocks.

The Amazonian giant centipede can grow to more than 30 centimetres (1 foot) long and has claws that secrete toxic venom.

Children at a nursery in Weston-super-Mare, England, were alarmed to see a three-headed, six-legged mutant frog creep out of their pond. They were told off for fibbing when they got home.
(Only kidding!)

A Labrador dog was badly injured when it tried to lick up biscuit crumbs that had fallen into a home paper shredder in Scotland. The shredder was activated, trapping the poor pooch's tongue.

Elephants have been known to stay standing up after they have died!

Garra rufa fish are used in some health spas to treat skin disorders. People sit in pools full of the 'doctor fish' and wait for their dead skin and scabby bits to be nibbled away.

A hunter from the Basque village of Epelette was shot in the hip when one of his dogs stood on a loaded gun in the back of his car.

The Barents Sea is teeming with monster Kamchatka crabs. The gigantic crustaceans can measure more than 1 metre (3 feet) from claw to claw and can weigh up to 12 kilograms (25 pounds).

The spiny Australian lizard *thorny devil* will put its head between its front legs if threatened. A second, false head then pops up for the predator to munch on instead.

The African *zorilla* could be the smelliest creature on the planet. The pong secreted from its anal glands can be detected one kilometre (half a mile) away.

A vet was hospitalized with hydrogen sulphide poisoning after entering a cottage that had 20 cats locked inside. The toxic fumes were from the cats' faeces.

When a male lion takes over another lion's pride, he will kill any cubs so that he can later replace them with his own. Not very good step-fathers!

Kangaroo manure has been used to make environmentally friendly paper in Tasmania.

The carrion beetle loves a tasty snail as a snack. It squirts digestive juices over the shell and then sucks out the snail's body. Delicious!

An elephant can produce a 38-kilogram (83-pound) pile of poop in one go.

The jewel wasp lays its egg inside a cockroach, using a paralyzing sting to keep it still. The hatched larva then munches on the cockroach's internal organs until it becomes a wasp and bursts out.

A giant catfish in a park lake in Germany became known as 'Kuno the killer' after it jumped out and ate a Dachshund puppy whole!

British man Michael Fitzgerald needed plastic surgery on his legs and arm after he was attacked by a badger at his home in Evesham, England. The badger attacked four more people before it was caught.

Some stinkbugs can spit their smelly goo as far as 30 centimetres (1 foot).

The New Zealand *huhu* beetle is otherwise known as a 'haircutter'. It has sharp hooks on its long legs and antennae, so if one lands in your hair and gets entangled you need a haircut to get it out!

Since the mid 1990s, many Tasmanian devils have died from *devil's facial tumour disease*, a mysterious illness in which large tumours around and inside the mouth prevent feeding, causing the animals to die of starvation.

A cow called Punch urinated on British celebrity Bill Oddie while he was doing a live broadcast from a farm in Scotland.

The Australian navy boarded an Indonesian ship that was drifting off the northwest coast and found that there was no crew but 3 tonnes (6,614 pounds) of rotting mackerel and tuna onboard.

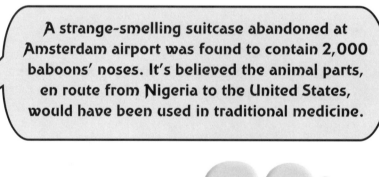

A strange-smelling suitcase abandoned at Amsterdam airport was found to contain 2,000 baboons' noses. It's believed the animal parts, en route from Nigeria to the United States, would have been used in traditional medicine.

Glassfish are transparent so you can peer in and see their bones and internal organs!

Wild boar hair was used to make toothbrushes before more hygienic, synthetic bristles were invented.

Cow parts caused traffic chaos when a meat lorry crashed near San Francisco and scattered its cargo across the freeway.

Cone snails or *cone shells* kill their prey by firing a poisonous harpoon from their mouths. Their venom is highly toxic to humans, who unknowingly pick up the pretty shells. The harpoon is so sharp that it has been known to penetrate wetsuits.

Hyenas have extremely acidic digestive juices. This means they can digest every bit of their prey, including teeth, hooves and horns.

An iguana's teeth are almost transparent.

South African man Abel Manamela took revenge on the bank that repossessed his car by releasing deadly adders into the building. As a cleaner was bitten by one of the snakes, he was charged with attempted murder.

The polar bears in Singapore Zoo turned green in 2004. Their change in colour was due to a type of algae growing in their hollow hair shafts.

A *scatologist* is a person who studies animal faeces.

Honeybees will surround any intruder in their colony, such as a hornet, and vibrate their bodies. This creates so much heat that the invader is cooked to death!

British anti-litter campaigners have warned that junk food litter is creating monstrous 'super-pigeons' that rely on waste to survive.

Cows produce 200 times more saliva than humans. What a lot of dribble!

A sparrow was shot dead in a hall in Leeuwarden, Holland, after sending more than 23,000 dominoes tumbling over. The dominoes had been set up for a world record attempt and the organizers were a little annoyed.

Rat's urine often carries *Weil's disease*, a serious and sometimes fatal infection that causes jaundice and kidney damage. It is usually contracted after contact with infected water.

A two-headed turtle hatched at a turtle refuge in Costa Rica. It was believed that the deformity was caused by ocean pollution.

Bad-tempered hippos kill more people in Africa than any other big-game safari animal, including crocodiles. They usually charge and trample victims, but have also been known to bite a man's head off!

A giraffe's blue-black tongue is *prehensile*, meaning it can grasp things. It can be as long as 60 centimetres (2 feet)!

The venom of recluse spiders is *necrotic*, which means a bite will result in a large, open sore that will take months to heal and may require skin grafts.

The word bonfire comes from 'bone fire', since ritual fires usually involved the burning of animal bones to ward off evil spirits.

Slugs produce two sorts of mucus: one is thin and watery, the other is thick and sticky.

British artist Chris Ofili is known for using an unusual ingredient in his paintings: elephant dung!

The fat-tailed scorpion is responsible for most human deaths from scorpion stings. Although its venom is less toxic than that of the deathstalker scorpion, it injects more into its victim.

The violet gland is a tail gland in foxes and badgers used for scent marking. The gland's secretion is fluorescent in ultraviolet light and although it contains the same substance as violet flowers, it is far more concentrated and smells really nasty.

If a predator gets too close to a vulture, it will protect itself by trying to vomit in the predator's eyes, causing a burning sensation.

Stampeding wild pigs killed Indonesian footballer Mistar during a 1995 training session.

Bombardier beetles protect themselves from a predator by blasting an explosive fart of boiling hot poisonous gas in its direction.

A common cause of pet ferret deaths is the reclining chair. The ferret snuggles up under the chair when it is reclined and then gets squished when its unknowing owner puts the seat back in position.

Bee sting therapy is sometimes used to treat conditions such as multiple sclerosis and arthritis. Bee venom contains a substance called *melittin*, which is anti-inflammatory (reduces swelling). Bees are pressed on to the patient and allowed to sting.

Animal dandruff is called *dander*.

British performance artist Paul Hurley wrapped himself in clingfilm and wriggled about in a soggy field nibbling soil for nine days. He called his performance *Becoming Earthworm*.

The Mexican mountain village of Atascaderos was plagued by rats that had learnt to avoid poison. It was estimated that there were 250,000 rats roaming the village.

The hairy-handed crab has hairy pads on its nippers where food particles collect. When it's hungry, the crab nibbles on its hairy claws!

The tiny black and white *minute pirate bug* bites by sticking its beak-like snout into the skin.

Pilobolus is a fungus that grows on herbivore dung and breaks it down. Although less than 1 centimetre (1/4 inch) tall, it can launch its *sporangium* (spores) up to 2 metres (6 feet) away. The herbivore eats the sporangium with the grass and the cycle begins again.

The skin and feathers of *pitohui* birds are poisonous. Touching them will cause numbness and tingling.

When animal control officers in Virginia investigated complaints of a foul smell coming from the house of pensioner Ruth Kneuven, they found over 300 cats, more than 80 of which were dead.

A snow scorpion is used to such low temperatures that one would die from heat exhaustion if you held it in your hand. As if you'd want to!

The number of cane toads in Australia reached a record 200 million in 2006. The army was called in to help control the plague of poisonous amphibians.

Rats cannot burp or vomit – but they can spread disease.

Three Peruvian fishermen who were lost at sea for 59 days survived by eating turtle meat and drinking turtle blood.

Kangaroos cover themselves with saliva to keep cool in the scorching Australian sun.

Research by scientists Dr Ben Wilson and Dr Bob Batty revealed that herrings fart frequently… but only at night!

A skunk can squirt its sulphurous spray up to 3 metres (10 feet) away, leaving its victim with stinging eyes and gasping for air.

Porcupines looking for salt have been known to eat tool handles and clothes because of the salty human sweat on them.

When Romanian Gyenge Lajos complained to the authorities about a gas-like smell, investigators soon discovered the cause: a dead cow in the man's apartment. It had been a gift from a friend and the man was cutting pieces from it as he needed them.

The Chow is the only breed of dog that has a purple-black tongue.

South American silk moth caterpillars are extremely venomous. They are covered with hairs that release anticoagulant venom on contact, so that an affected person can bleed to death.

The largest known jellyfish is the Arctic *lion's mane* jellyfish. The biggest ever found was washed up in Massachusetts Bay; its body was a huge 2.3 metres (7 feet 6 inches) wide and its tentacles were 36.5 metres (120 feet) long.

Customs officials at Melbourne airport were suspicious when they heard splashing sounds coming from a woman's skirt. Further investigations revealed that she was smuggling 51 live tropical fish in a water-filled apron.

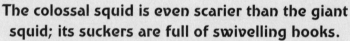
The colossal squid is even scarier than the giant squid; its suckers are full of swivelling hooks.

The giant squid has hundreds of suckers and inside each one is a ring of sharp teeth, so it can suck on to its prey and perforate it at the same time.

A monstrous wild hog dubbed 'Hogzilla' was shot in the state of Georgia in 2004. It was 2.4 metres (8 feet) long with 23 centimetres (9 inch) tusks.

The male funnel-web spider is extremely aggressive. It will actively attack a person by lunging and will bite repeatedly.

A decomposing sperm whale exploded in Taiwan as it was being transported for a post mortem, showering nearby shops and cars with blood and blubber. A natural build-up of gas inside the beached whale was to blame.

A giraffe's heart is 60 centimetres (2 feet) long and weighs around 11 kilograms (25 pounds).

The red 'blood sweat' that a hippopotamus secretes contains sunscreen and antibacterial agents. The secretion starts off clear and changes colour to red, then brown.

The Australian *fierce snake* has the most toxic snake venom in the world. A single bite contains enough venom to kill up to 100 adult humans.

Once a year, the roads and paths of Christmas Island are covered with red crabs that are scuttling from their burrows towards the sea to lay their eggs. There are so many that cars just have to drive over them.

The pearl fish swims into a sea cucumber's anus and lives inside it during the day, coming out at night. The sea cucumber breathes through its anus, so it can't keep the fish out!

The glass frog has a transparent body – its blood vessels, stomach and beating heart are all visible.

A scorpion can go for a whole year without eating.

There are more than 70,000 types of slug and snail in the world. Let's hope they never hold a big party!

Some spiders spit special sticky goo at their prey so that it's literally glued to the spot.

As cockroaches grow, they develop a new skin inside their old one, eventually splitting the old one. This new skin is white until it hardens in the air and becomes dark.

The viperfish has teeth so long it can't close its mouth and it has to open its jaws out flat before it can swallow. Its teeth are half the length of its head!

A mosquito can drink one and a half times its own weight in blood at a single meal. Yuck!

The skin of a hippopotamus measures about 4 centimetres (1.5 inches) thick. That's about 3.5 centimetres (over an inch) thicker than human skin.

Bone-eating zombie worms live on the decaying bodies of dead whales. They have no gut, but bore deeply into the bones. Microbes inside the worms digest chemicals sucked out of the bones.

The banded tenrec, a kind of hedgehog from Madagascar, sometimes eats so many worms, bugs and slugs that it makes itself sick.

Sharks will eat almost anything. The stomachs of dead sharks have been found to contain bits of boats and vehicles and once, several hundred years ago, even a knight in armour.

If a rat didn't keep chewing, its lower teeth would eventually grow through its top jaw and up into the roof of its mouth.

A shark can detect blood over a kilometre (about half a mile) away.

In the time of the dinosaurs, there were giant scorpions nearly a metre (3 feet) long. That's bigger than the average domestic dog!

Every year, 4.5 million litres (1 million gallons) of dog urine is peed in London's parks.

A spider that isn't hungry will wrap up extra bugs in its web to keep for later.

There are 3,500 known species of cockroach. Are there others out there? We just don't know yet…

Dracula ants, discovered in Madagascar in 1993, practise cannibalism, punching holes in their own larvae and feed off their blood.

In the USA, Dan Aeschleman's business is selling fox urine. Farmers buy it to keep animals away, as they smell the urine and think a fox is near.

Carrying garlic might repel mosquitoes rather than vampires.

Flesh flies eat nothing but old meat and rotting flesh on dead bodies.

A planarian worm will regrow its other half if cut in two. If two planarians are cut in half, they can be mixed up and re-attached to the wrong half.

The blobfish lives at great depths and looks just like… a blob. Its body is a jelly-like mass.

Some geckos have no eyelids – they lick their eyeballs to clean them!

The Romans used crushed mouse brains as toothpaste.

The vampire squid has the largest eyes of any animal for its body size. The squid is 28 centimetres long (11 inches) and its eyes are 2.5 centimetres (1 inch across). The equivalent would be a person with eyes the size of table tennis bats!

The job of guard termites is to defend the termite nest or mound. Sometimes they explode in their efforts to deter attackers.

A duck-billed platypus can stuff its cheek pouches with 600 worms.

Female Egyptian vultures are attracted to the male with the yellowest face. Unfortunately for the males they have to eat their own poo to achieve this look!

Around four times a year, adult toads will shed their skin then eat it.

The southern giant petrel, a bird that lives near the South Pole, spits globs of oil and regurgitated food at its enemies.

The leopard seal sometimes attacks people, lunging up through the ice to snap at their feet.

The carpet viper kills more people in the world than any other type of snake. Its bite leads to uncontrollable bleeding.

Cockroaches taste through their feet.

A baby naked mole rat has transparent skin – you can see its insides right through its skin!

Copepods are tiny crustaceans that swim around in groups of up to a trillion. They are the only known creature that has just one eye.

The wood frog that lives in the Arctic Circle can stay deep-frozen for weeks and survive.

Sharks don't have a urinary tract so their urine leaks out of their skin.

Bored monkeys will throw their faeces at anyone who happens to be passing!

Nose bots are maggots that live inside the noses of animals that graze, such as sheep, cows and horses.

The Gila monster is a lizard from South America and Mexico. Although it's only just over half a metre (2 feet) long, its bite is so strong that the only way to detach one that's bitten you is to drown it.

A rat can fall from a five-storey building and walk away unharmed.

Rats have super-strong teeth. Amongst other things, they can bite through wood, metal and electric cables.

A cockroach can survive being frozen in a block of ice for two days.

The only mammals that don't get lice are anteaters, armadillos, bats, duck-billed platypuses, whales, dolphins and porpoises.

The deep-sea gulper eel can eat fish larger than itself. It can open its mouth so wide that its jaw bends back on itself at an angle of more than 180 degrees.

The caterpillar of the polyphemus moth in North America eats 86,000 times its own birthweight in the first 56 days of its life. It's equal to a human baby eating 270 tonnes (nearly 600,000 pounds) of food!

The bulldog ant from Australia will sting again and again while holding on with its fierce jaws. It can kill a human in 15 minutes.

The fart of a female southern pine beetle contains a pheromone called *frontalin*, which attracts male beetles.

The curly heaps of earth you find on the ground outside are called worm casts. They are actually little piles of worm poop.

Chameleons can change their skin colour to hide themselves (camouflage) – but they also change colour according to mood. Some turn grey when depressed.

Head lice suck blood for about 45 seconds every 2–3 hours, but they can go without a meal for up to two days if they are between heads – on a comb, towel or pillow.

Instead of eyelids, some geckos have a transparent coating over their eyes. It stays permanently closed but allows the gecko to see anyway.

A kind of yellow-bellied toad can produce a nasty foam that smells of garlic to deter attackers.

Komodo dragons are lizards 3 metres (10 feet) long. They aren't poisonous, but there are so many bacteria in their mouths – growing in rotten meat between their teeth – that a bite from one often leads to blood poisoning and death.

The naked mole rat is perhaps the ugliest mammal in the world. It looks like a wrinkly sausage with very short legs and huge, protruding teeth. It has no hair anywhere except the inside of its mouth.

The bluebottle and greenbottle flies common in houses lay their eggs in rotting meat, dead animals and animal faeces.

Bracken Cave in Texas is home to 20 million bats. The floor is caked in a thick layer of bat faeces.

Only female mosquitoes bite and suck blood – they need the protein in blood so that they can lay eggs. The males only eat nectar from flowers.

Crows are one of the few larger creatures that eat rotting and putrid flesh.

A maggot doesn't have teeth – it oozes a kind of spit called *ferment* onto its food. This dissolves the food, and the maggot then sucks it up.

A hissing cockroach makes a noise by squeezing air out of tiny holes in its body segments. The sound can be heard 3.7 metres (12 feet) away.

The axolotl is a pale amphibian that is partway between a tadpole and a lizard, and lives in a single lake in Mexico. Some axolotls change shape and become land creatures, but most don't ever change.

Baby Komodo dragons will eat their brothers and sisters if they are hungry and there is no other food.

If an octopus loses a tentacle, it can grow a new one.

An octopus tentacle will carry on wriggling for some time after being cut off.

A stingray has a special cap on the end of its tail which breaks off when it stings, allowing poison to pour out into the wound it's made in its victim.

Bat faeces lie so deep on the floors of their caves that people harvest them to sell as fertilizer for plants.

The aye-aye is a nocturnal mammal from Madagascar that has one very long, bony finger on one hand. It looks so frightening that local people believed contact with an aye-aye led to death, so they killed most of them.

Mosquitoes have been around for 200 million years. That's so long that even dinosaurs could have been bitten by them!

Flies beat their wings about 180 times a second.

The guanay cormorant makes its nest from dried faeces.

The anglerfish has a glowing blob attached to a spike at the front of its head. In the dark, deep sea the glowing blob attracts small prey which the anglerfish then sucks in and gobbles up.

In South Africa, termites are roasted and eaten as snacks, just like popcorn.

Flies eat by vomiting up something they've eaten previously so that the chemicals in their vomit can start to dissolve the new meal. When it's sloppy, they suck it all up again. That's why it's a really bad idea to eat anything a fly's been sitting on!

Sharks have special organs in their snouts and elsewhere that let them detect the electric fields produced by living animals. They can then home in on the animals to eat them.

Plagues of flying foxes (fruit bats) can destroy a fruit orchard in a single night.

The face fly feeds on the mucus produced in a cow's eyes and nostrils.

A giraffe has special valves in its arteries so that its blood can be pumped up to its head. Without them, it would need a heart as big as its whole body!

Land leeches in Asia can drop from trees onto people and suck out so much blood the person dies.

A cockroach can withstand more than 120 times the force of the Earth's gravity – an astronaut passes out at 12 times the pressure of gravity.

Slugs are attracted to beer! Some gardeners trap them by putting out bowls of beer which the slugs fall into. They get drunk and drown. The slugs, not the gardeners…

A 32-kilogram (70-pound) octopus can squeeze through a hole the size of a tennis ball.

The end of a chameleon's tongue has a club-like lump oiled with sticky goo, which helps it to catch insects.

The Australian blue-ringed octopus can pump out a poison that will paralyze or kill a human.

Goliath bird-eating spiders can grow to the size of a dinner plate and kill small birds.

When there's not much food around, cockroaches will eat each other – ripping open the victim's stomach and tearing out the insides.

Some toads can swallow shrews and mice whole.

A head louse can lay 200–300 eggs during its life of around 30 days. The eggs only take five to ten days to hatch and start feeding.

Over 100 million years ago, crocodiles were twice the size they are now – up to 12 metres (40 feet) long – and could eat dinosaurs.

Baby cockroaches feed on their parents' faeces to get the bacteria they need to help them digest plants and vegetables.

Geckos and centipedes both eat cockroaches.

A full-grown python can swallow a pig whole.

Chocolate can be deadly to a dog's heart and nervous system. Just a handful is enough to kill a small dog.

If a lizard loses its tail, it can grow a new one.

A patch of rainforest soil around the size of this book can hatch 10,000 mosquito eggs.

Rabbits partially digest the grass they eat and then excrete it as soft, gluey pellets. They then eat these to finish digesting their meal properly.

Crocodiles carry their young around in their mouths.

The geographic tree frog can change its eyes from brown to patterned to help it camouflage itself in trees.

When a viperfish wants to eat a large meal, it moves all its internal organs towards its tail to make more room inside it for food.

> **Light-coloured spots on surfaces of food show that a fly has vomited something up and tasted the surface; dark-coloured spots are fly faeces.**

An elephant normally produces around 23 kilograms (50 pounds) of faeces every day.

Vampire bats drink half their body weight in blood every day.

Cat urine glows in the dark (but it has to be very dark, if you're thinking of testing it).

A ribbon worm can eat 95 per cent of its own body and still survive.

A cockroach can live for a week after its head is cut off.

When a fish called the Pacific grenadier is pulled out of the sea by fishermen, the change in pressure makes gas inside it expand quickly and its stomach pops out of its mouth.

Dogs in New York City produce 18 million kilograms (40 million pounds) of faeces a year. Luckily, New Yorkers have to clear up after their dogs.

A leech will suck blood until it is 10 times its original size and can't hold any more. Once it's full, it drops off its victim.

A vampire finch in the Galápagos Islands pecks holes in other birds to feed on their blood.

Leeches don't only suck from the outside of your body. If you drink water with a leech in, it can attach to the inside of your mouth or throat and, in a river, leeches can go into your bottom and suck you from the inside.

The gavial, a kind of crocodile from India, has over 100 teeth.

The potato beetle larva protects itself from birds that want to eat it by covering itself in its own poisonous faeces.

The turkey vulture excretes faeces
onto its legs to keep them cool.

**The female
black widow spider
eats the male after
mating, sometimes
eating up to 25 partners
a day. Now *that's* a
man-eater!**

A chameleon's tongue can be twice
as long as its body, and must be
kept curled to fit inside its mouth.

A baby robin eats 4 metres
(14 feet) of earthworms a day!

When a toad is sick, it vomits up its own stomach,
which hangs out of its mouth for a short time
before it swallows it back down.

**Some
leeches have
three mouths,
with up to
a hundred
teeth.**

Many leeches produce a pain-killer so that you don't notice you have been bitten unless you actually see the leech.

The queen naked mole rat is the only one to have babies. She keeps the others sterile (incapable of having babies) using a special chemical in her urine.

A very stressed octopus will sometimes eat itself.

Body lice love dirty places – they were very common in the old days when people didn't wash much, and they often infested soldiers who had to live in dirty conditions. They are most likely to live on your tummy or your bottom.

A female German cockroach can produce 500,000 young in a year.

Crocodiles can't bite and chew. Instead, they hold their prey under water to drown it, then twist their bodies around to tear chunks off the victim.

In some types of anglerfish, the male is much smaller than the female and attaches himself to her body for life. After a while, he becomes fused to her and their body systems combine. His only role is to fertilize her eggs, and he is nourished by her blood.

Roger Dier of Petaluna, California, USA, really liked rats. The trouble was that he kept 1,300 of them all in his one-bedroom flat!

Vampire bats urinate the whole time they're sucking blood. This ensures they don't get so full of blood they're too heavy to fly. So, smarter than a vulture, then!

A dustbin can produce 30,000 flies a week from eggs laid in the rotting rubbish it contains.

The slime eel, or hagfish, feeds on dead and dying fish at the bottom of the sea. It goes into its victim through the mouth or eye socket and eats it away from the inside, leaving only a bag of skin and bones.

The venom of the brown recluse spiders is a *necrotic*, which means a bite will result in a large, open sore that will take months to heal and may require skin grafts.

Whales have been found with circular scars on their skin – marks from the suckers of giant squid.

Scorpions paralyze their prey before they suck the juices out. It's not dead, but it can't escape.

The female praying mantis begins to eat the male during mating; he carries on, but she eventually eats all of him.

When the *necrophorus* beetle finds a small dead animal, it pushes it into a suitable place, takes some of its fur to make a nest and lays its eggs near the body. When the eggs hatch into maggots, they feed on the dead body.

Bird parents eat food for their babies, fly back to the nest and vomit up the meal into the babies' open beaks.

A chicken once lived 10 days after a French farmer cut its head off. He fed it with a dripper, directly into its throat.

Vampire bats don't suck – they make a cut in their victim, then lick the blood as it flows out. To keep it flowing, they have an *anticoagulant* in their spit – a chemical which stops blood from clotting and forming a scab.

Some types of octopus contain a poison which instantly kills anything that eats it.

The pharaoh ant likes to live in hospitals where it feasts on wounds, bloody bandages and IV solutions.

African dung beetles eat animal faeces. Five thousand beetles can eat a pound of faeces in two hours.

A single female fly can hatch up to 1,000 babies (maggots) in her lifetime.

A lamprey is like an eel but has no jaws. Instead, it has a sucker-like mouth with rows of teeth. It attaches itself to a fish, digs itself in and then sucks all the fluids out of the fish, eventually killing it.

Head lice have two sharp mouthparts – one cuts through your skin and sucks up blood, the other pumps out spit containing a chemical that stops your blood clotting.

Soldier flies like to lay their eggs in human faeces. The larvae (maggots) are often found in bathrooms as they crawl up the sewage pipes.

Cockroaches breed so fast that if all the young survived and reproduced, there would be 10 million cockroaches from a single pair by the end of a year.

A shark will eat parts of its own body that have been cut off or bitten off by another animal.

Scorpions can withstand extremes of temperature and even radiation. A scorpion could be frozen in a block of ice for three weeks and walk away unharmed, and survive 200 times the dose of radiation that would kill a person!

Some types of baby Australian spider bite limbs off their mother to feed on over several weeks.

Some leeches can suck enough blood in one meal to keep them alive for nine months.

Horn flies attack bulls – as many as 10,000 can land on a bull's back and suck its blood until it dies.

Locusts, like giant grasshoppers or crickets, travel in swarms of up to 80 million and each eats its own weight in plants every day.

The Japanese beetle found in Canada and the USA can eat through a human eardrum.

Cows partly digest the grass they eat, then vomit it back up into their mouths and chew and swallow it all over again. That's what they're doing when you see them chewing in a field when they're not munching on a fresh mouthful of grass.

The female hissing cockroach surrounds her eggs with a frothy substance that hardens; she then carries them inside her body for two weeks until they hatch.

If one vampire bat is too ill to leave the cave, another will suck blood all night then come home and vomit it up for the sick bat so it doesn't miss out on a meal.

The *death's head hawkmoth* has a skull-shaped pattern on its back. It is believed in many cultures that it brings bad luck if it flies into a house.

The butcher bird (shrike) impales mice, small birds and lizards onto spikes to hold them still while it eats them.

An elephant's trunk is so handy that it can pluck a single blade of grass from the ground.

South American cane toads have special glands behind their eyes which ooze poison out of their skin. They can even shoot the poison up to 30 centimetres (nearly a foot) to deter animals that might want to eat them.

A jellyfish excretes faeces through its mouth. It has only one opening and uses it for all purposes.

Cockroaches have an oily coating to make them slithery.

If you're bitten by a moray eel, the only way to get it off is to kill it, cut the head off and break the jaws. It won't let go while it's alive.

There are over 3,000 different types of mosquito and they live all over the world, even in the coldest places near the North and South Poles.

Aardvarks and anteaters enjoy nothing better than slurping up ants and termites with their long, sticky tongues.

Driver ants and army ants both march in massive colonies and will strip to the bone any animal they come across. They'll even tackle a wounded crocodile or lion that can't get away. Driver ants slash at their victims who eventually bleed to death from thousands of tiny cuts.

Flies have 1,500 tiny taste hairs on their feet so that they can taste what they are standing on.

Inuit people have to cover all exposed skin with a thick layer of mud to avoid fierce biting flies in the summer.

A starfish can turn its stomach inside out, pushing it out through its mouth opening.

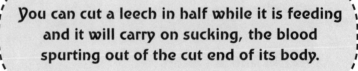

You can cut a leech in half while it is feeding and it will carry on sucking, the blood spurting out of the cut end of its body.

Fossilized cockroaches 300 million years old have been found. This means they were around 100 million years before the dinosaurs evolved!

A flea can jump up to 220 times its own body length – a flea the size of an adult human could jump over a 25-storey building and more than a 0.4 kilometre (a quarter of a mile) along the ground.

The armadillo produces so much spit that it has a special reservoir to store it in.

A grotesque frog which can turn from green to beige often lives in letterboxes and toilet bowls in Australia and New Guinea.

Rats that hibernate together sometimes get their tails tied up in a knot. If they urinate over themselves in the winter, they can freeze together in a block. A knot of rats is called a king rat.

A giraffe can lick inside its own ears.

Some leeches only suck the blood from dead animals.

When a turtle (which is immune to jellyfish stings) eats a Portuguese man-of-war jellyfish, it produces a smell that attracts sharks – so the jellyfish eventually gets its revenge!

Eye gnats are attracted to the moisture produced by your eyes and nose. In the USA, they are a common nuisance on hot summer evenings. They lay their eggs in rotting vegetable matter or animal faeces.

Termites fart out between 20 and 80 million tons of gas every year (not each, all together).

Flea larvae eat their parents' faeces — or each other.

Scorpions sometimes eat their own babies.

The horned lizard from South America shoots blood out of its eyes when it is attacked. It increases the blood pressure in its sinuses until they explode, spraying blood onto the attacker.

The African clawed toad lays up to 10,000 eggs, but many of its tadpoles are deformed. The parents eat the deformed ones when they hatch.

The slime eel or hagfish produces slimy mucus from pores in its body. If something disturbs it, it throws out strings of mucus which makes the sea around it jelly-like, gunky and impossible to swim through. They can suffocate on their own slime if they overdo it.

Octopuses sometimes remove stinging tentacles from jellyfish and use them as weapons.

A praying mantis is an insect rather like a cricket, but up to 12 centimetres (5 inches) long. It can kill and eat small lizards and birds, holding them impaled on a special spike it has developed for the purpose. A really hungry mantis will eat its own babies.

Cockroaches can make themselves super-slim and can flatten their bodies to a size just a little thicker than a piece of paper to crawl into cracks.

When an opossum is threatened, it plays dead, lying still with its tongue hanging out, and excretes faeces on itself and oozes green slime that smells of rotting flesh.

A flea can jump 30,000 times without stopping.

When a large batch of mosquito eggs hatches all at once, the babies might all attack the same unfortunate animal wandering past. They can suck it dry and kill it, if it's a small animal and there are enough mosquitoes.

The echidna is a mammal which lays an egg and keeps it in a pouch on its stomach.

The pouch grows just before the female produces the egg and disappears again after the baby has left it.

The babies of the Surinam toad grow under the mother's skin on her back. They stay there for up to 130 days.

The eyes of a chameleon can move separately, so it can look in two directions at once.

The deep-sea anglerfish can stretch its stomach to swallow prey much larger than itself.

Some types of botflies lay their eggs on the abdomen of another blood-sucking insect such as a flea or tick. The eggs hatch while the host feeds the larvae and burrows into the skin of the animal it's sucking on.

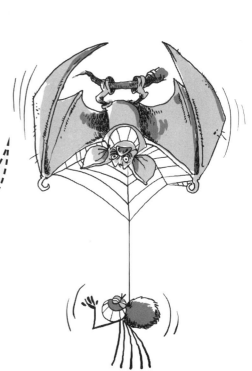

Three-toed sloths move so slowly that algae often grows on their fur.

Planarian worms shoot a tube out of their throats which holds down their prey. Then they drip enzymes all over their victim to soften it up before tearing chunks off it to eat.

Leatherback turtles have spines in their throats! They stop their favourite snack of jellyfish from sliding back out of their mouths.

The Dracula fish has no scales but makes up for this lack with a set of fangs that would make Drac himself green with envy.

A crocodile's digestive juices contain so much hydrochloric acid that they have been found to dissolve everything from iron spearheads to large steel hooks.

If a shark gets turned onto its back, it goes into a state of paralysis for up to 15 minutes.

A mummified dog was found inside a tree 6 metres (20 feet) above the ground in Georgia, USA. The hollow tree was the perfect condition to keep the dog preserved for 20 years after its death.

An octopus has to turn itself inside out to eat, as its mouth is hidden in between its tentacles.

A group of jellyfish is called a 'smack'.

Jackals will eat diseased or decomposing flesh even if it has been rotting for days. They will feed their pups with their own vomit to prevent starvation. If the pups get too full, the jackals will just eat their regurgitation.

Pet food manufacturers once developed a mouse-flavoured cat food, but cats just didn't like the taste.

The female tahr (a relative of the goat) from India lets the male know she is ready for mating by urinating on him. Nice!

Electric eels can deliver a shock of 500 volts to stun their prey into submission. The electricity supplied to your home is only 240 volts!

One of the favourite dishes of Japanese Emperor Hirohito was rice cooked with wasps. Spicy!

The tentacles of the deadly box jellyfish contain tiny harpoons which inject poison into its unlucky victim.

Scientists have created genetically engineered mice whose hearts flash green when they beat. They'd be great fun at parties!

A frog juice market stall in Lima, in Peru, offers visitors a refreshing drink of skinned frogs blended into a smoothie. The locals claim this tasty treat cures a range of illnesses.

The jaws of a snapping turtle are so powerful that they can rip off a human finger.

Dogs have been known to sense that their owner will suffer an epileptic seizure up to an hour before it actually happens.

Mosquitoes love stinky human feet because of the enzymes found on them.

Siberian Huskies can live and work in temperatures as low as -60 degrees Celsius (-75 degrees Fahrenheit).

The stonefish is one of the ugliest fish around and also one of the most dangerous. Its sting is excruciating and can be fatal.

Turkeys have been known to have heart attacks. When the US Air Force began tests to break the sound barrier they found entire fields of turkeys on the flight paths dead from the shock of the sonic booms.

A woodpecker's tongue can be as long as its body! It has a barb on the end of it for skewering grubs. Yummy!

While sleeping, humans swallow an average of 14 bugs per year.

Some owls can turn their heads round at a 270-degree angle. They have to do this because their eyes are too large to move in their eye sockets.

Vultures sometimes eat so much that they become too heavy to fly. They have to vomit to bring their weight down again.

A Hindu temple dedicated to the rat goddess Karni Mata in Deshnoke, India, houses more than 20,000 rats.

The Giant Isopod is a huge sea woodlouse that can grow to a length of 36 centimetres (46 inches). It munches on dead and decaying fish.

Large rodents called Agoutis are the only animals that can open brazil nuts with their teeth.

Until 1997, the punishment for killing a panda in China was death.

A giant anteater gobbles up around 3,000 ants and termites in one day, using its sticky tongue that can be as long as 60 centimetres (2 feet)!

New Zealand fisherman caught a colossal squid that was 10 metres (30 feet) long. Its body was so enormous that *calamari rings* (squid rings) made from it would be as big as tractor tyres!

It can take a month for the contents of a sloth's stomach to digest completely.

Hoatzin chicks from South America can climb trees. They use special claws to move around until their wings are strong enough for them to fly.

Beavers have a set of transparent eyelids to protect their eyes as they swim underwater.

Dachshund means 'badger dog': the dogs were originally bred for killing badgers, rabbits and foxes. Not so cute, then!

The only fruit eaten by aardvarks is known as the *aardvark cucumber*. African Bushmen call it *aardvark dung*!

Bedbugs and fleas can live for a whole year without eating.

The feathers of a pigeon weigh more than its bones!

Two smelly musk hogs were married in a lavish ceremony in Taiwan to celebrate the Year of the Pig. The pigs were dressed up for the occasion and even got to scoff some wedding cake!

If you keep an albatross on a boat, it can get seasick.

A starving mouse will eat its own tail.

Never kill a hornet near its nest. If it sends out a distress signal, all the hornets in the nest may come out to attack.

A four-legged duckling was born on a duck farm in Hampshire, England. The farm owner named him Stumpy.

When it attacks prey, the great white shark rolls its eyes backwards to protect them.

When it's time for dinner, a spider traps its prey before injecting it with a chemical that turns the bug's insides to mush. The spider then sucks out the liquid like a bug milkshake.

If salamander larvae detect tadpoles swimming in water around them, their bodies develop to become much stronger. They also grow flatter heads, making them killer predators.

The Argentinian wide-mouthed frog has a mouth so wide that it can eat prey as large as itself.

A 12-month-old baby was saved at the Hadassah hospital in Jerusalem in 2004 after a snake attack. The boy survived because his nappy absorbed most of the venom.

The world's population of termites expels up to 79 billion kilograms/176 billion pounds of gas every year. That's 34 times more than the human population!

Scorpions glow a yellowy-green colour under ultraviolet light.

The giant cricket of Africa enjoys eating human hair. Nobody really knows why!

Toxoplasma is a parasite that lives in rats' brains, changing their brains to make them less scared of cats. This means the rats are more likely to be caught and eaten, helping the parasite to move easily into cats' brains – their favourite place of all.

The number of mosquitoes that hatch during the Arctic summer is so great that their swarms blot out the sun.

The highly prized Malaysian liqueur habu sake is made from fermented viper venom.

Cockroaches taste with their feet.

Ailurophobia is aear of cats. Julius Caesar, Henry II, Charles XI, and Napoleon were all sufferers and would nearly faint in the presence of a cat.

Only female mosquitos drink human blood. They do it to get the protein they need to lay eggs.

Meerkats are immune to many deadly venoms and will eat scorpions … stinger and all!

The *candiru* (an eel-like fish) can smell urine in water. It heads straight for the source, enters its victim's body and feeds on its blood.

A fly's eye blinks at five times the rate of a human eye. If a fly watched a movie, it would see it as a series of still photographs.

If you are getting eaten by something big, green and full of teeth, the chances are it's a crocodile; alligators don't like the taste of humans.

The *tarantula hawk* is actually a wasp! The female attacks and paralyses a tarantula so that she can lay her egg on its body. The hatched larva then eats the tarantula alive.

King snakes, such as the king cobra, eat other snakes.

According to an old Californian law, it is illegal to pile horse manure more than 1.82 metres (6 feet) high on any street corner.

The babies of the *boulengerula taitanus* (a worm-like amphibian) eat their own mother's skin. The babies use special teeth when born to squirm all over their mother's body and remove her flesh. Somehow the mother usually survives!

To keep themselves cool, some tortoises urinate on their back legs. The evaporating liquid helps take away body heat.

Just a single bat can eat between 3,000 and 7,000 mosquitoes in a night. A colony of 500 of the flying fiends can munch their way through a quarter of a million bugs in an hour.

A python can live for a whole year without eating anything.

Fuji the dolphin put on weight after having her diseased tail amputated because she couldn't swim properly. Handlers at the Japanese aquarium came up with a speedy solution – a new tail was made from the material used for Formula One racing car tyres!

Parrotfish can make themselves a kind of mucus sleeping bag! It masks their smell from predators and keeps parasites away.

The poisonous copperhead snake smells like freshly cut cucumber. Just don't put one in your salad!

When staff at the British Museum saw the first duck-billed platypus, they thought it was a fake animal and tried to pull off its bill!

The burrowing owl makes its nest underground and lines it with cow dung.

When in unfamiliar territory, a hamster will rub its scent glands (found along its sides) against various objects. This leaves a scent trail the hamster can follow in order to come back the other way!

A rhinoceros's horn is not a true horn – it's made of matted hair.

Being trampled by a cow is the cause of death for around 100 people each year.

Swordfish have special organs in their heads that heat up their eyes and brain.

Because of the position of their eyes, rabbits can see behind them without turning their heads.

An Australian crocodile was so annoyed by the sound of a chainsaw nearby that it ran at the man using it and grabbed it from him!

Using a powerful magnet, it is possible to make a small frog lift off the ground and stay suspended in the air. Don't try it at home!

If they are injured or damaged, newts can re-grow body parts, including legs, arms and even a new heart!

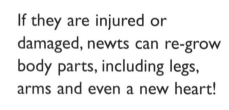

A rattlesnake's venom remains poisonous up to 25 years after it has died.

The *Polynesian skink* (a small lizard) has a bright blue tail which it can shed if it is attacked. The tail carries on wriggling after the lizard has gone, keeping the predator distracted.

A tiny tree frog wandered into the freezer of a café in Darwin, Australia, and was found frozen solid. Once thawed out, though, it was fine.

A porcupine can swallow 100 times the amount of poisonous hydrogen cyanide that is needed to kill a human – and suffer no ill effects.

Meat-eating animals won't eat an animal that has been struck by lightning.

The *mabra elephantophila* moth drinks the tears of elephants. The moth actually makes the elephant cry by dragging its proboscis (needlelike snout) across the elephant's eyeball.

Jokers who let a rat loose in a British McDonald's branch were taken aback when the restaurant manager beat it to death with a broom in front of customers.

The cassowary bird's dagger-like middle claw is 12 centimetres (5 inches) long and razor sharp, enabling the bird to disembowel an enemy with a single kick.

Whales vomit every 7–10 days to get rid of any indigestible items they may have swallowed. It's not known if they warn any nearby sea creatures what's coming.

Hard ticks (ticks that have shells) that burrow in to people's skin can spread *Rocky Mountain spotted fever*, originally known as black measles. It causes fever, muscle pain, headache and a rash. If untreated, it can be fatal.

When a kodiak bear kills a deer, it will eat the internal organs first.

Horrible History Facts

Queen Victoria's coronation ring was made for her little finger, but the Archbishop of Canterbury insisted on forcing it on to her ring finger to follow tradition. The Queen was in agony during the ceremony and it took two hours to get the ring off afterwards.

King George II died of a heart attack while he was on the toilet.

Roman gladiators in training were fed spoonfuls of ash by their trainers, in the belief that it built up the body. So don't moan again about eating your greens…

Scottish aristocrat Alexander Hamilton, the tenth Duke of Hamilton, wanted to be mummified after his death and so bought an ancient Egyptian sarcophagus. When he died in 1852, his legs had to be shortened to fit his body inside it!

Charles VI of France suffered from a mental illness that made him believe his body was made of glass. He even put metal rods in his clothes so he wouldn't shatter.

The dead bodies of poor people who couldn't afford funerals were often thrown in the nearest river. Dredger men were paid for each corpse they collected.

French watchmaker Robert Hubert was hanged for starting the Great Fire of London, but it was later discovered that he arrived in the city two days after it broke out. He confessed to the crime, so was either tortured or a bit mad.

In the 16th century, combs were often made from elephant's tusks (ivory).

When he was badly injured in the First World War, author Ernest Hemingway stemmed the flow of blood with lit cigarette ends.

Poor Victorians used to mix flour with water to make baby food. Unsurprisingly, babies were often sick in those days.

During the 18th century, fur used for hats was soaked in a solution containing high levels of mercury. The toxic vapours caused mercury poisoning, a symptom of which was *dementia* – that's where the phrase 'as mad as a hatter' came from.

Mircea, the brother of Vlad (when he was just Vlad and hadn't yet started impaling) was blinded with hot stakes and buried alive by his enemies.

English King Edward the Martyr was killed by his stepmother in 979 AD. She offered him a drink and then stabbed him in the back as he sat and drank it.

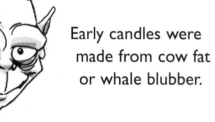

Early candles were made from cow fat or whale blubber.

Scottish writer Sir Thomas Urquhart literally died laughing! This cause of death is known as 'fatal hilarity'.

The guillotine is associated with the French Revolution, but a similar device called the *maiden* was used in Scotland long before that. It was introduced by James Douglas, fourth Earl of Morton, who ended up being executed by it himself for treason.

Glue used thousands of years ago was made by boiling up animal hooves and leaving the goo to set. You had to break the hooves up into chunks first.

Viking funerals often involved putting the corpse in a boat and setting fire to it.

Many men and horses died during the chariot races popular with the ancient Greeks and Romans. Death was all part of the fun in those days!

Old shipwrecks are often riddled with *shipworms*, snaky molluscs that burrow into the wood and chomp away at it.

Most medieval manuscripts were written on bits of stretched out calf-skin, known as *vellum*.

The Tower of London's famous ravens all died of shock during the Second World War bombings of London. A new flock was put in place before the Tower reopened.

Russian writers Alexander Pushkin and Mikhail Lermontov both died from gunshot wounds after fighting in duels.

An unusual duel to the death was fought in Paris in 1808: two Frenchmen shot at each other from hot air balloons until one balloon was shot down!

It was believed in the Middle Ages that if you had some of your enemy's hair, you had control over him (or probably just his head lice).

In 212 BC, 460 Chinese intellectuals who refused to burn their books during the Qin dynasty were buried alive for their defiance.

Animal blood was believed to have special powers and was often sprinkled on the statues of Norse gods. People taking part in these rituals would often shower themselves with the blood too!

The first *bone china* was made with crushed ox bones.

When Viking warlord Ragnar Lodbrok was defeated during a battle in England in 865, he was thrown into a pit of venomous snakes and bitten to death.

The deteriorating mummy of pharaoh Ramesses II was sent to Paris to be treated for a fungal infection (mould) in 1974. It was issued with a passport for transportation on which the occupation was stated as 'King (deceased)'.

English mathematician Alan Turing committed suicide by painting an apple with cyanide and eating it.

In 200 BC, Carthaginian soldiers pretended to flee their city and left behind wine laced with the toxic plant *mandrake*. Invading Romans guzzled the wine, only to be finished off by the returning soldiers while they were weakened by the poison.

King Harold was killed at the Battle of Hastings in 1066 by an arrow shot through his eye.

For two years after the Krakatoa volcano erupted in 1883, the moon appeared to be blue.

In the late 19th century, an Egyptian farmer discovered a tomb that was filled with thousands of mummified cats and kittens.

The hot summer and unprecedented levels of sewage in the Thames in 1858 led to The Great Stink – Londoners were almost knocked out by the foul smell.

There were hundreds of altars for animal sacrifices at the ancient Greek Olympics. The biggest of these was the Great Altar of Zeus, where the thighs of 100 oxen would be roasted for the gods. The other bits were used for a big banquet later.

Black pox was a symptom of smallpox, in which the skin took on a charred appearance, turning black and peeling off.

People afflicted with warts during the Middle Ages used to pay a wart-charmer to get rid of them.

Renaissance painters coated their canvases with rabbit-skin glue, made from boiling rabbit skins. It was all they could think of to prepare their paper for oil paints!

The *Scavenger's Daughter* was a 16th-century torture device that compressed the body until blood came out of the nose and ears.

During the embalming of Catherine of Aragon's body, her heart was found to be black. This led to fears that she had been murdered, but it is more likely that it was a form of cancer.

In the 8th century, Chinese poet Li Bai drowned in the Yangtze River when he drunkenly tried to touch the moon and fell in!

When the Bishop of Rochester's cook poisoned some guests, Henry VIII chose the punishment: the cook was boiled alive in his own pot!

Before shoe polish was invented, people would make their shoes waterproof by rubbing them with a lump of sheep fat.

Realizing that he had become extremely unpopular, King Henry I of Haiti shot himself with a silver bullet in 1820, rather than go through the indignity of a coup.

Men of the Iron Age were sometimes buried with their chariot...
along with the poor horses that pulled it.

Ivory black paint wasn't just any old black paint – it was made by burning an elephant's tusk, scraping off the black bits and mixing them with oil.

An English ship, *The Mary Rose,* sank in 1545. It wasn't recovered until 1982, when the remains of half the crew were found on board.

The victorious enemies of Roman emperor Valerian killed him by pouring molten gold down his throat.

German scientist Georg Richmann heard a thunderstorm in 1753 and rushed out to observe it. Lightning collided with his head, his shoes exploded and he died.

Italian dictator Benito Mussolini was expelled from school at the age of 11 for stabbing a schoolmate in the hand and poking a stick in another boy's eye.

On American ships, cats with extra toes were thought to bring good luck on voyages. In Europe, it was believed that cats with extra toes belonged to witches and should be destroyed!

People suffering from tuberculosis during the 17th century were thought to be vampires, since they were pale, had swollen, bloodshot eyes and coughed up blood.

In his later years, Chairman Mao Zedong had green teeth!

Arsenic was a popular murder weapon in the Middle Ages; as well as being tasteless and colourless, it resulted in the same symptoms as cholera and often went undetected.

In the late 19th century, most public places in the United States had *spittoons*, which were dishes for men to spit into. It was thought to be more hygienic than spitting on the floor.

Whenever the Kodiak people (Alutiiqs) killed a bear, they would leave the head as a sign of respect for the spirit of the bears.

Dutch artist Vincent van Gogh had such a bad diet (bread, coffee and absinthe) that his teeth were loose. He looked so scary, especially after he cut off part of his ear, that neighbours petitioned to have the *fou roux* (the mad redhead) removed.

Early thickeners for inks included the sludge from boiled-up donkey skins and insect faeces.

On realizing their impending defeat, several high-ranking Second World War Nazis killed themselves with cyanide salts. The poison would have quickly caused convulsions before death.

Egyptian queen Cleopatra killed herself by deliberately taking figs from a basket that also contained venomous asps (snakes). She kindly allowed two of her handmaidens to die with her.

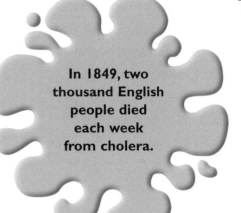

In 1849, two thousand English people died each week from cholera.

Tightly-laced corsets that were fashionable between the 16th and 18th centuries would squeeze the internal organs; the liver would be pressed against the ribs, the stomach was made smaller and the lungs would not be able to work properly, leading to a build-up of mucus and a persistent cough.

A medieval cure for just about anything was *cauterization*: the affected body part was burned with a hot poker.

The toxic plant *mandrake* was used as an early anaesthetic by the Romans to make patients drowsy, so they didn't feel a limb being amputated… quite as much!

The first American astronaut Alan Shepard had to urinate inside his spacesuit after his Mercury capsule flight was delayed for several hours.

For thousands of years, crushing by elephant was a common form of execution in parts of Asia.

American president George Washington suffered with his teeth. He had several different sets of dentures made for him, including one set made from human and cow teeth set in a metal base. The result of eating too many sweets, George?

The *blood eagle* was a particularly gruesome Viking method of murder. Whilst still alive, the victim's ribs would be cut and opened out, then the lungs would be removed.

After Prince Albert's death, Queen Victoria insisted that fresh clothes be laid out for him every day. This continued to be done for 40 years after he died.

The *retarius* was a Roman gladiator who fought by catching his opponent in a huge lead-weighted net before moving in for the kill with a trident.

Seven hundred black bears were killed and skinned in order to make Busby hats for the soldiers at Queen Elizabeth II's coronation in 1953.

Victorian women rubbed a concoction of arsenic, vinegar and chalk into their skin in the belief that it kept their skin youthful. Wrinkles? Maybe not. Arsenic poisoning? Definitely!

Brutal Roman Emperor Caracalla was assassinated by one of his own officers... while urinating at a roadside.

Medieval foot soldiers used huge, sharp forks to spear passing knights and pull them off their horses.

Any Roman gladiators who tried to stop fighting would be prodded with hot pokers to spur them on again.

Bolshevik revolutionary Leon Trotsky was murdered by a blow to the skull with an ice axe from a Stalinist agent.

As long ago as 1000 BC, Indians inoculated themselves against smallpox by rubbing pus from the pustule of an infected person into a scratch on a healthy person. The Chinese did it by blowing powdered smallpox scabs up the noses of healthy people.

The ancient Phoenicians discovered that they could get purple-blue dye from the mucus of sea snails.

Part of Lincoln Park in Chicago was previously a cemetery. Although it was believed that the graves had all been moved, skeletons were still being discovered during construction work in the 1980s.

When Coca Cola was first invented in 1885, it was a medicine made with the illegal drug cocaine.

In ancient Greece, prisoners condemned to death were made to drink a solution made from the toxic plant *poison hemlock*. The most famous victim was the philosopher Socrates.

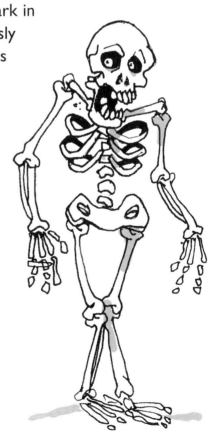

Mary Ann Cotton was a 19th-century serial killer who used arsenic to fatally poison up to 20 people, including her own husbands and children. She was hanged for the murders but died a slow, painful death after the hangman misjudged the dropping distance.

Holes in Viking longships were plugged with a sticky mixture of tar and animal hair.

Part of a human skull discovered next to a pub car park in Crewe, England, was identified as being 700 years old. Fancy waiting that long to be served!

An ancient Persian method of execution, known as *the boats*, involved covering the condemned criminal in honey, tying him to a boat and leaving him on some stagnant, smelly water to be eaten alive by insects.

French king Charles I was killed by the single stroke of a *halberd*, an axe on a pole that was sharp enough to slice right through the steel helmet that he was wearing.

The *Death Railway* that linked Thailand and Burma was built by the Japanese during the Second World War. More than 100,000 labourers and prisoners of war died during its construction.

Unwilling to live under Caesar's rule, Roman statesman Cato the Younger tried to kill himself with his sword. He failed and was stitched up by a doctor, but then pulled the stitches out and ripped out his own intestines.

Research on Beethoven's hair showed that he died of lead poisoning. That's probably why he was as deaf as a post!

After the French ship *Medusa* ran aground in 1816, those who escaped on a raft resorted to cannibalism after four days adrift.

Early 19th-century Scottish surgeon Robert Liston could carry out an amputation in just 30 seconds. Since there were no anaesthetics in those days, it was just as well!

Murderous dictator Idi Amin, known as the Butcher of Africa, used a hotel in Kampala as his interrogation and torture centre.

After he was killed by the French at the Battle of Trafalgar, Horatio Nelson's body was preserved in a barrel of brandy for transport to London. He wouldn't have been too happy if he'd known it was French brandy!

American writer Sherwood Anderson died after swallowing a toothpick.

King Henry I of England's son William drowned when the *White Ship* sank in 1120. The ship's owner would have survived, but when he discovered the heir to the throne had died, he drowned himself – the King would have killed him anyway.

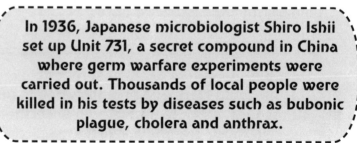

In 1936, Japanese microbiologist Shiro Ishii set up Unit 731, a secret compound in China where germ warfare experiments were carried out. Thousands of local people were killed in his tests by diseases such as bubonic plague, cholera and anthrax.

The earliest examples of tuberculosis were found in 17,000-year-old bison remains.

Richard the Lionheart died from an arrow wound that became gangrenous in 1199. His intestines were buried in Châlus – the place where he was shot with a crossbow – his heart in Rouen in France, and the rest of his body at Fontevraud Abbey in Anjou, France.

The great sword or long sword used in medieval battles was so big that it had to be held in both hands. It could chop off a limb, even through armour.

Henry II of France was killed during a jousting match when the sliver of a shattered lance pierced his eye and brain, coming out near his ear.

Ancient Romans used whips with pieces of bone or metal on the end. A plain old whip just wasn't nasty enough!

Chinese Prime Minister Li Si invented the *Five Pains* execution: a condemned prisoner had his nose, hand, foot and testicles cut off before being sawn in half. Li Si got his comeuppance, because he ended up being executed this way in 208 BC!

In 1920, Ray Chapman became the only Major League baseball player to have been killed by a pitch (a bowled ball). The sound of the ball hitting his skull was so loud that one player mistook it for the ball being hit with the bat and fielded it.

A lot of the ancient Greek Olympic events were done in the nude. (Try not to think of all those wobbly bits!)

So many people died from the Black Death that funerals were dispensed with and infected bodies were thrown into 'plague pits'. Pits were often filled with hundreds of corpses.

Women used to apply eye drops made from deadly nightshade to make their pupils bigger, in the belief that it made them look more beautiful. In fact, the toxic drops blurred their vision, increased their heart rate and if used often, caused blindness.

Rather than fall into enemy hands, Samurai warriors would commit suicide by *seppuku*, slicing open their stomachs with their sword in the belief that their spirit would be released.

Soviet leader Vladimir Lenin spent the last six years of his life with a bullet lodged in his neck, left there after an assassination attempt. He would never get through customs these days.

In 1936, the United States was hit by a deadly heatwave which killed around 20,000 people. The victims died of heat stroke and heat exhaustion when their body temperature soared out of control.

Sir Francis Drake died of *dysentery* (the mother of all diarrhoeas!).

The punishment for 17th-century French murderer Marquise de Brinvilliers was to be force-fed 9 litres (16 pints) of water before being beheaded. They burned her at the stake too, just to be sure.

The terrifying 15th-century warrior Pier Gerlofs Donia was known for his ability to chop off several enemies' heads with one swing of his great sword.

As a boy, Spanish artist Salvador Dalí was horrified to find his pet bat dead and covered in ants. He later used ant images in much of his work.

In 18th-century France, it was traditional to remove and preserve the hearts of dead monarchs.

Allan Pinkerton, the founder of the first US detective agency, slipped in a Chicago street and bit his tongue. He didn't seek treatment and died of the infection that followed.

Sweating sickness was an infectious disease that killed thousands of people in Europe during the 15th and 16th centuries. Violent shivers and severe neck pain would be followed by excessive sweating and delirium.

Each newborn baby in the ancient Greek city of Sparta was bathed in wine and then taken to the elders, who would decide if it was strong enough to be reared. If not, it was left on a hillside to perish. That's one way to stop a baby crying!

Chinese Emperor Qin Shi Huang took mercury pills to give him eternal life. Unfortunately, they gave him mercury poisoning and killed him instead.

The unluckiest of gladiators had to fight as an *andabatus*. They were on horseback but were made to wear helmets with no eyeholes, so they couldn't see what was coming.

Abraham Lincoln's mother died after drinking milk from a cow that had eaten *white snakeroot*, a poisonous herb. *Milk sickness* killed many people in the 19th century.

Italian-French composer Jean-Baptiste de Lully stabbed himself in the foot with his long baton while conducting a work for Louis XIV. An abscess formed but he refused to have the gangrenous toe amputated, and later died of blood poisoning.

The *morning star* was a medieval club-like weapon with big spikes on the end. It was used to kill or wound the enemy with the double whammy of a heavy blow and piercing them with a spike.

Baking powder in the 19th century contained bone ash, the powder left over when animal bones were burned.

Nazi doctor Josef Mengele experimented with changes in eye colour by injecting chemicals into children's eyes.

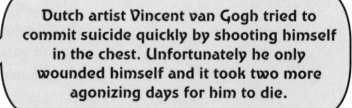

Dutch artist Vincent van Gogh tried to commit suicide quickly by shooting himself in the chest. Unfortunately he only wounded himself and it took two more agonizing days for him to die.

The old English occupation of *dog whipper* involved sitting in a church with a whip and using it to get rid of any unruly dogs that might disrupt the service.

The decapitated head of Vlad the Impaler was sent to Istanbul, where the Sultan had it preserved in honey and put on display as proof of the brutal Romanian's death.

Between 50 and 100 million people died from flu during a pandemic in 1918–1919, wiping out entire towns in some countries. Symptoms included blueness in the face and coughing up blood and bleeding from the ears.

A mini tsunami swept along the Bristol Channel, England, in 1607. Whole villages were swept away, with 2,000 people losing their lives.

Many medieval knights fighting in hot countries were known to have died of heat exhaustion, literally cooking inside their armour (especially the fatter ones!).

Josef Stalin was badly scarred by smallpox and had photographs touched up to hide the scars.

Following an argument over where English novelist Thomas Hardy should be laid to rest, his heart was buried in Dorset and his ashes in Westminster Abbey.

The dead body of King Harold II had to be identified in 1066 by the tattoos on his chest, as his face was so badly mutilated. The tattoos read 'England' and 'Edith'.

The last execution of a prisoner at the Tower of London was in 1941. German spy Josef Jakobs was shot by a firing squad of eight Scots Guards. As he already had a broken ankle, he was allowed to remain seated to receive his punishment in comfort!

During times of war, Japanese women would kill themselves before invading soldiers reached them. Using the method of *jigai*, they would cut their own throats.

Ancient philosopher Pliny the Elder was so keen to see Vesuvius erupting that instead of fleeing, he stuck around and ended up being killed by its poisonous gases!

Mexican artist Frida Kahlo was impaled though the abdomen by an iron handrail in a bus crash when she was 18 years old.

Anaemia (iron deficiency) was common amongst ancient Egyptians. It was caused by bloodsucking parasites such as hookworm, which were rife in those times. Tiny holes in the skulls of ancient Egyptian mummies are a telltale sign.

As a test of their masculinity, Spartans held competitions to see who could take the most flogging.

Some ancient Greek prisoners were executed in a *brazen bull*: they would be locked inside a brass sphere and a fire was lit underneath it, roasting the prisoner to death.

In ancient Roman funeral processions, jesters called *archimimes* were employed to walk behind the dead person and impersonate them (as they were when they were alive, obviously; a corpse impression wouldn't be that entertaining!).

During the Middle Ages, dead bodies that had to be transported over long distances were de-fleshed: skin, muscles and organs were cut away so that only the bones were left.

In France in the late 1600s, it was considered a great honour to talk to King Louis XIV while he was on the toilet.

In Anglo-Saxon times, shepherds were given 12 days' worth of cow manure at Christmas.

Vikings used rancid butter to style and dress their hair.

Biological warfare has been used since 600 BC when the Greek city Cirrha was besieged by Solon. He poisoned the water supply with hellebore roots, and then stormed the city while the citizens were weak from diarrhoea, having drunk the contaminated water.

During the 900 days of the siege of Leningrad in the Second World War, 1,500 people were accused of cannibalism.

The Greeks played the game knucklebones with real bones from the knuckles of animals with cloven feet – such as pigs, goats and antelopes.

In Palestine 8,000–9,000 years ago, a dead relative was buried under the floor of the family's house – except the head. The flesh and brain were removed from the head and the skull used as the base for a plaster mould of the person's head, which was decorated and kept.

After a massacre carried out by Indian soldiers in 1857, the British soldiers made the Indians clean up the blood – and those who refused had to lick it up.

Franz 'The Flying Tailor' Reichelt designed a huge overcoat that doubled as a parachute. He demonstrated his invention in 1912 by jumping off the first deck of the Eiffel Tower, but it didn't work and he fell to his death.

The Inuit people used to make trousers out of the gullets – windpipes – of seals or walruses, using one for each leg.

Theban king Mithradites (132–63 BC) took small doses of poison regularly to develop immunity and protect himself from poisoners. When he later wanted to kill himself, the poison he took did not kill him.

Wig makers suffered during times of plague as people thought the disease could be caught from wigs made of human hair. So many secondhand wigs were infested with fleas that they were probably right!

Many children who had to work underground in mines in the early 20th century lost their eyesight from being in darkness all day.

Toad eaters were people employed by men selling medicine at fairs and markets. The toad eater had to swallow a toad – supposed to be deadly poisonous – and then take the medicine. Their survival encouraged people to buy the medicine. They may or may not have actually swallowed the toads...

Victorian child chimney sweeps sometimes had to crawl through chimneys as narrow as 18 centimetres (7 inches). If they didn't go quickly enough, their bare feet were pricked with burning straws.

Birching was allowed as a punishment in Britain until the 1940s. It consisted of being beaten on the bare buttocks with a bunch of twigs.

In ancient Egypt, women kept a cone of grease on their head. During the day, it melted in the hot sun and dripped down, making their hair gleam with grease.

The cork false leg of 19th-century Mexican general Santa Anna was captured by US troops and is on display in a museum in Illinois.

During the Great Plague that struck England in 1665–66, boys at Eton school were punished for not smoking, as smoking was thought to protect them from the disease!

In the 19th century, a school headmaster in York, England, massacred his pupils and hid their bodies in cupboards.

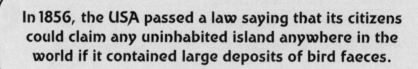

In 1856, the USA passed a law saying that its citizens could claim any uninhabited island anywhere in the world if it contained large deposits of bird faeces.

Mary Stuart, queen of England from 1553 to 1558, had 274 people burned at the stake just for being Protestant Christians.

Pope Clement VII tried eating a death cap toadstool in 1534; it killed him.

Before written or computerized records helped us to keep track of criminals, many countries marked criminals with a tattoo or a branding iron – a red-hot iron was used to burn a pattern, letter or picture into their skin. This meant that everyone could see what they had done.

Bird faeces called *guano* were collected and sold from Peru, Chile and Bolivia for hundreds of years. It was used as a fertilizer for plants.

Ancient Egyptian mummies frequently still have their fingerprints intact, as the hot conditions of their desert tombs dried out the flesh and preserved them.

The Greek emperor Draco died when he was smothered by the hats and cloaks that admirers threw over him at a party.

It took over two months to make an Egyptian mummy. After removing the internal organs and brain, the body was covered with a kind of salt for two months to dry out, then treated with resin, packed with sand and sawdust and wrapped in bandages.

Mongol leader Tamerlane the Great (1336–1405) executed anyone who told him a joke he had already heard.

In 2350 BC the Mesopotamian king Urukagina demanded that thieves be stoned to death with stones carved with their crime.

Roman prisoners condemned to fight to death with each other or wild animals often tried to kill themselves before the fight. One man pushed a wooden spike down his throat – it was used for holding the sponge people cleaned themselves with in the bathroom.

Anglo-Saxon peasants sometimes wove clothes made out of dried stinging nettles.

Anyone who rebelled against the Mesopotamian king Ashurnasirpal could expect to be skinned or buried alive. We know this because he buried some rebels inside a column and carved the story of their crime on the outside.

In ancient Rome, vestal virgins were young girls who served in a temple and could not be touched. If they committed a crime their punishment was to be buried alive as it could be carried out without anyone touching them.

The Romans had criminals torn apart by wild animals while the public watched. Dogs or lions were usually used, but sometimes more exotic animals were brought into the arena.

In the time of King Charles II of England, who reigned from 1649 to 1685, dead people had to be buried in a shroud made of wool, to boost business for the wool trade.

In Anglo-Saxon England, people who died in a famine were eaten by their neighbours!

The scarab beetle was treated as holy by the ancient Egyptians. Scarab beetles roll themselves in a ball of faeces and lay their eggs in it.

The Roman king Tarquin crucified anyone who committed suicide – even though they were already dead – to show other people what would happen to their bodies if they did the same.

In 1740, a cow found guilty of witchcraft was hanged.

A medieval trial of guilt required a suspected criminal to plunge their hand into a pan of hot water and take out a stone, or carry a red-hot iron bar. The injured arm was bandaged and inspected after three days. If it was healed the person was considered innocent. If not, they were guilty and were punished.

In 167 BC, a Roman commander had a group of soldiers trampled to death by elephants for deserting (running away from battle).

The Mongolian ruler Ghengis Khan imposed the death penalty for urinating in water because water was so precious in the Mongolian desert.

The Spanish Inquisition was set up to find people who committed crimes against the church and its teachings. They often questioned and tortured people until they confessed. In the case of a child under 10, they could go straight to the torture and not bother with the questions.

Lord Nelson (1758–1805) admiral of the English fleet, slept in a coffin in his cabin. The coffin was made from the mast of an enemy French ship.

During the time of Henry VIII of England, who reigned from 1508 to 1547, the punishment for poisoners was to be boiled alive.

To make violin strings, the gut of a sheep – which could be up to 30 metres (over 98 feet) in length – was removed intact. The blood, flesh and fat were then scraped off the outside, any half-digested grass was squeezed out and the gut was washed out carefully. The wider end was used for sausage skins, the rest for violin strings.

In India, people used to believe that the eyes of a slow lorris – a nocturnal creature like a monkey with no tail – could be used in a love potion.

An ancient Egyptian cure for burns involved warming a frog in goat dung and applying it to the burn.

When Sir Walter Ralegh was executed in 1618, his wife had his head embalmed. She carried it around with her for 29 years, until her own death.

The Roman emperor Valerian was captured by Visigoths (a barbaric tribe) when they invaded Rome in 260. They skinned him alive and then displayed the skin as a sign of their triumph.

Ancient Greeks used to blow up a pig's bladder like a balloon and use it as a ball.

An Anglo-Saxon cure for baldness was to rub the ash from burnt bees into the head.

Greedy Swedish monarch King Adolf Frederick's biggest meal consisted of lobster, caviar, kippers and cabbage, followed by 14 servings of his favourite dessert. It was to be his last – he died shortly afterwards of digestion problems.

A French medieval torture involved trapping a person in the stocks – a wooden structure that held the ankles of the victim, who was seated on the ground – and pouring salt water over their bare feet so that a goat could lick it off.

The Hungarian countess Elizabeth Bathori killed more than 600 young girls in the 1500s in order to drink and bathe in their blood.

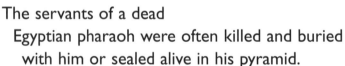

The servants of a dead Egyptian pharaoh were often killed and buried with him or sealed alive in his pyramid.

The poet Shelley drowned off the coast of Italy in 1822. His body was washed up, half eaten by fish, and cremated on the beach by his friends. One of them cut his heart from his burnt body and gave it to Shelley's wife, who kept it all her life.

Hanging, drawing, and quartering was a punishment for the worst crimes in England from 1241. First the prisoner was nearly strangled by hanging, then cut open, had his innards removed and cooked in front of him, and finally was chopped into four pieces. By the mid-1700s, prisoners were killed before the drawing and quartering stages.

Capuchin Monks in Sicily, Italy, embalmed the dead and stored them in the catacombs in Palermo. Around 6,000 mummified bodies, some seated or standing, can now be visited by tourists who come to the city.

A Saxon cure for madness was a beating with a whip made from the skin of a dolphin.

Ancient Egyptians sometimes brought a mummified body to banquets to remind diners that one day they would die.

Early colonists in America used to clean their windows with rags dipped in urine.

In the Middle Ages, butchers often killed animals for meat in their shops, then threw the innards out into the street.

Fashionable women in Japan and Vietnam stained their teeth black until the mid-1900s.

Romans who killed a relative would be executed by being tied in a sack with a live dog, cockerel, snake and monkey and thrown into a river.

Wool used to be softened by people trampling on it in a large vat of stale (two-week-old) urine and ground clay. The people who did this were called 'fullers'.

During a famine and drought in 1609 in Jamestown, USA, one settler was executed for eating his dead wife.

A dead body found in the Alps in 1991 was at first thought to be a climber who had died. Investigators discovered it was a man who had been mummified naturally in the ice after dying 5,300 years ago. They named him Otzi.

So many people associated with the discovery of Otzi have died young that some believe the mummy is cursed.

The Incas of South America used to mummify their dead kings and leave them sitting on their thrones.

People hunting animals examine the faeces of their quarry to find out information about the size, sex, and type of animal. In the Middle Ages, hunters often carried the faeces around with them while they hunted, storing them in their hunting horns.

Queen Christina of Sweden, who reigned from 1640 to 1654, had a miniature cannon and crossbow for executing fleas.

French actress Sarah Bernhardt took a coffin with her on all her travels. She learned her lines while lying in the coffin and even entertained her lovers in it.

In the 1700s, people wore huge hairstyles made of a mixture of real hair and horse hair or other fibres. Kept in place for months on end, they were rarely cleaned, so sticks had to be used to knock out any vermin that decided to set up home in the hairstyles.

Sailors in the olden days often had a single gold tooth, which could be pulled out and used to pay for their funeral if they died away from home.

An Egyptian mummy can be covered in more than 20 layers of bandages, with glue between each layer. Every finger and toe was wrapped separately. It took 15 days to wrap a royal mummy.

In the 1700s, European women had their gums pierced so that they could fit hooks to hold their false teeth in place.

Ancient Romans made hair dye from pigeon faeces.

Uruguay's rugby team was stranded in the Andes in South America after a plane crash in 1979. It took 70 days for them to be rescued, and they had to eat the other passengers who had died in the crash.

An ancient Egyptian who was feeling a bit unwell might eat a mixture of mashed mouse and faeces. Mmmmmmm, bound to make you feel better!

In 1846, 87 pioneers crossing the mountains of California, USA, became trapped in bad weather. By the end of the winter, 40 of them had been eaten by the others.

King Pepi II of Egypt had himself surrounded by naked slaves smeared with honey so that any biting flies would be attracted to them and not bite him.

In the 1800s, flea circuses were popular – the fleas were glued into costumes and stuck to wires or each other to look as though they were performing tricks.

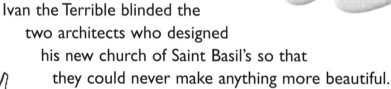

Mongolian leader Tamerlane played polo using the skulls of enemies killed in battle.

Ivan the Terrible blinded the two architects who designed his new church of Saint Basil's so that they could never make anything more beautiful.

The Russian ruler Peter the Great had his wife's lover decapitated and insisted that she keep his head in a jar of alcohol beside her bed as a reminder of her crime.

In China, in the 1500s, a common method of committing suicide was by eating a pound of salt.

Vlad the Impaler, ruler of Transylvania, had over 20,000 enemies impaled on spikes between 1456 and 1476.

The word *thug* comes from 'Thuggees', who were an Indian cult – sometimes described as the world's first mafia – who used to trick and murder people as human sacrifices to their goddess Kali.

In Europe, between the 12th and 17th centuries, Egyptian mummies were ground up and used in medicines.

In the Middle Ages, people made washing powder from wood ash and urine.

In the 1700s, fashionable European women commonly shaved off their real eyebrows and stuck on false ones made from mouse fur.

A Bohemian army general was so devoted to his country that when he died he asked for his skin to be removed and made into a drum that could be beaten in defiance of Bohemia's enemies. It was used nearly 200 years later at the start of the Thirty Years' War in 1618.

British king James I's tongue was too large for his mouth, so he slobbered all the time and was a very messy eater.

Charles I was executed by beheading, but had his head sewn back on so that his family could pay their respects to his body. His doctor stole a bone from his neck and had it made into a salt cellar.

In 1981, 300 people thrown into the water in a ferry accident in Brazil were eaten alive by piranhas.

London prisoners condemned to death used to go to chapel on the Sunday before their execution where they had to sit around a coffin while the priest told them how sinful they were.

In times of famine, Stone Age tribes would eat old women before dogs – they thought them less useful.

The body tag from the corpse of Lee Harvey Oswald, who shot President John F. Kennedy, was sold for £3,600 at an auction.

James, Duke of Monmouth, was beheaded in 1685. But when it was discovered that there was no official portrait of him, his head was stitched back on and he posed for his portrait at last.

The 15th-century German king Wenceslas was so angry with his chef after a particularly bad meal that he had him roasted alive.

Saint Ignatius of Antioch prayed to be eaten by wild animals; when the Roman emperor Trajan sentenced him to be eaten by lions in AD 110 Saint Ignatius fell to his knees and thanked him.

In 896, the rotting body of Pope Formosus was removed from his coffin, dressed in his papal robes and put on trial. Found guilty, his blessing finger was cut off and he was thrown in the river.

The body of British philosopher Jeremy Bentham was preserved and kept in an open wooden box, which is still on display at University College, London. For many years, Bentham was brought out to attend special functions and meetings.

Russian leader Peter the Great had a museum in which he kept the stuffed bodies of deformed people and animals, such as a child with two heads and a sheep with five feet. The museum was looked after by a deformed dwarf who knew he would become an exhibit when he died.

It took the executioner three blows to behead Mary, Queen of Scots, in 1567. And he still had to saw through the remaining skin and gristle with a knife.

The body of Roman gladiator and slave rebel leader Spartacus was never found, but Roman general Crassus had 6,000 of Spartacus's followers crucified along the Appian Way, as a warning to any future rebels.

During the Reign of Terror following the French Revolution, 17,000 people were beheaded using the guillotine.

Scottish bagpipes were originally made from the entire skin or stomach of a dead sheep.

In ancient Egypt, a flea catcher would cover himself in milk and stand in the middle of a flea-infested room until all the fleas jumped onto him. He would then leave, taking all the fleas with him.

English hatmakers used to soften the straw they plaited into hats by spitting on it.

King Kokodo of the Congo ruled for three years after his death. His body was wheeled around in a box during this part of his reign…

In the 1800s, there were several cases of people being buried when not really dead. Terrible stories about opened coffins with scratch marks on the inside, and corpses with fingernails worn away by trying to escape, led to cautious people being buried with a system of warning bells fitted in the coffin which they could ring if they woke up.

During witchcraft trials in Salem, Massachusetts, USA, in 1692, 25 people were condemned to death on the flimsy evidence of a group of hysterical girls.

It is said that the cursed mummy of Egyptian princess Amen-Ra was on board the *Titanic* when it sank in 1912, killing 1,500 people. The mummy was being sent from the British Museum to the USA; only the lid of the mummy's coffin is still in the British Museum.

Ivan the Terrible of Russia punished a bishop by having him stitched into the skin of a dead bear and releasing a pack of hounds to hunt and kill him.

Bald Romans used to make a paste of mashed up flies and spread it over their heads in the belief that it would make their hair regrow. It didn't…

Instead of a hollow pumpkin with a candle inside, Celtic people are said to have used real human heads cut from the bodies of defeated enemies to keep away ghosts and ghouls.

In ancient times, a mixture of dog and chicken faeces was smeared on animal hides as part of the leather-making process. The smelly mess would be left for months before being scraped off with a knife.

In Europe, women would sometimes wear hollow sticks filled with sticky tree sap around their necks. The sticky substance was intended to attract and trap any fleas that were thinking about hopping on to the women.

The earliest cosmetic surgery was practised by doctors in India, who made fake noses for criminals whose noses had been cut off as a punishment for their crimes.

Chimney sweeps used to have three baths a year – one in the spring, one in the autumn, and one for Christmas. The rest of the time, they were covered in soot.

If sheep grazed on pastures full of clover, shepherds sometimes had to puncture the animals' stomachs with a sharp knife to release all the gases that built up inside them.

In the Middle Ages a royal farter was employed to jump around farting in front of the king to amuse him.

In the old days, a 'whipping boy' used to sit next to a prince during lessons. If the prince made a mistake, or did something wrong, the whipping boy was punished instead of the prince.

In Africa, it was common to bend back springy saplings and tie them beneath the ears of someone about to be beheaded, so that the person's last sensation would be of their head flying through the air.

A common test for the guilt of a person accused of witchcraft was to throw them in a pond. If they floated, they were guilty and were executed. If they sank, they were innocent – but probably drowned.

Until 1868, criminals could be transported from England and sent to Australia for 7–14 years as punishment for even petty crimes. The youngest victim was a boy of nine who was transported for stealing.

King Henry VIII of England used the death penalty more than any other English king in history.

In a punishment used in ancient China, a prisoner was locked in an iron cage with his head sticking out of the top. The cage was too tall to sit in and too short to stand up in. Some prisoners were left to starve to death in the cage.

At banquets, the Gauls used to award the legs of roast animals to the bravest warriors. Sometimes fights to the death resulted from the squabbles over who should get them.

Vlad the Impaler used to entertain guests to dinner surrounded by the bodies of people he had executed, impaled on spikes.

Long ago, criminals would be hanged in a metal cage called a *gibbet*, or in chains, near the scene of their crime until their bones rotted to nothing.

1577, an outbreak of typhus in a jail in Oxford, England, killed 300 people – including the judges, jury, witnesses and spectators at the criminal trials being held there. The prisoners, used to living in filthy conditions, all survived.

During the French Revolution, large crowds watched public executions by guillotine. People would rush forward to try to catch some of the blood as it dripped from the severed heads lifted to show the crowd. Many a bloody handkerchief was kept as a gruesome souvenir.

In 1857, a group of Indian people who rebelled against the ruling British were strapped across the mouths of live cannons and blown to bits when cannonballs were shot through them.

People who killed themselves used to be buried at a crossroads with a stake through their heart. It was thought that they couldn't go to heaven, and the crossroads would confuse their ghost so that it couldn't find the way home to haunt anyone.

A trusted servant of William of Orange, a Dutch king of England, spent money the king had given him for clothes on pistols, which he used to shoot the king. As punishment, he had his flesh pulled off with red-hot pincers, his guts pulled out, and his body cut into pieces.

Inca women washed their hair in week-old urine, braided it, and then used more stale urine to keep it in place.

The first person to be found guilty of a crime on the basis of fingerprint evidence was an Argentinian woman who murdered her children in 1892. Her fingerprints were found in blood on a door frame.

In ancient Babylon, a doctor who accidentally killed a patient had his hands cut off.

A punishment for an English woman who nagged her husband or gossiped too much was to wear a metal cage over her head called a 'scold's bridle'. It put a spiked plate inside her mouth that would cut her tongue if she moved it to speak.

In 1685, a wolf that terrorized a village near Ansbach in Germany was sentenced to be dressed in human clothing and hanged.

The Chinchorro people of Chile mummified their dead 8,000 years ago. They cut off the arms and legs, removed and smoked the skin, strapped sticks to the bones and replaced all the soft parts with grass and ashes, then put the whole body back together and painted it.

It is reported that during Napoleon's invasion of Russia in 1812, some soldiers cut open dead horses and sheltered inside them to avoid freezing to death.

During excavations at a circle of standing stones in Avebury, England, in 1938, archeologists found the body of a man who had been crushed under a falling stone in the 1320s when villagers had tried to bury the stones.

Over 100,000 people have been tried for witchcraft in Europe since 1100, most of them tortured and eventually executed.

English revolutionary Oliver Cromwell died of natural causes, but opponents had his body dug up, tried and executed. His head is kept in an unmarked location in Sidney Sussex College, Cambridge.

> **Some Stone Age people believed the spirit could only escape when the flesh had gone from the body, so they left corpses to rot or be eaten by wild animals, or hacked off the flesh, before burying them.**

As well as people, the ancient Egyptians mummified all kinds of animals, including cats, crocodiles, birds – even fish and dung beetles.

A 1,000-year-old grave in England was found to contain a rich woman in a coffin beneath a poor woman pinned down by a big stone. She was probably a slave, buried alive to serve the rich woman after death.

At the Aztec festival celebrating Xipe Totec – the Aztec god of spring – prisoners of war were flayed alive. Their skins were then worn ceremonially by priests to represent the renewal of earth and the start of new life in spring.

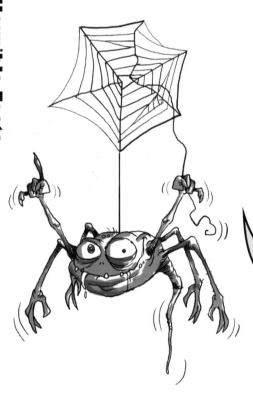

People of the North American Sioux tribe used to make an amulet of their own dried umbilical cord – the cord which connects the unborn baby to its mother's body – which they thought guaranteed a long life.

A Lhasa Apso dog was once imprisoned for biting, and kept on death row in a prison in Washington State, USA, for over eight years.

For nearly 1,000 years, Chinese women had their feet bound to keep them small. The toes were bent and the arch of the foot broken, and the feet were kept tightly bandaged from childhood until death. The practice was banned in 1911.

The ancient Britons used to practise euthanasia by jumping off cliffs to their deaths. If individuals were too elderly to jump they would be pushed!

In the 1700s, the penalty for wearing tartan or playing the bagpipes in Britain was death.

Anglo-Saxon parents were allowed to sell children up to the age of seven to be slaves 'if they needed to do so'.

British schools used to keep at least two types of standard cane for hitting naughty children. Children over 15 years of age could be hit with the senior cane, which was longer and thicker than that used on younger children.

People used to believe that smearing their clothes with fat from a dead pig would keep away fleas.

The Jivaros in the Andes shrunk the heads of enemies killed in battle. They skinned the head, then stitched up the eyes and mouth and stewed the skin for a couple of hours with herbs. Then they dried it, stuffed it with hot stones and sanded and polished it.

The internal organs of ancient Egyptians were kept in vases called *canopic jars*, labelled with hieroglyphics and figures. The figure of the baboon-headed god *Hapy*, for example, would be painted on a jar containing the lungs.

In the War of the Pacific (1879–1884), Chile fought against Bolivia and Peru over who was allowed to collect bird faeces and whether they should have to pay a tax on them.

Before modern plumbing, a gong scourer was a boy who was sent into cess pits to scoop and scrape all the muck into buckets and remove it. The job was so horrible it was done at night so that people wouldn't have to see it happening.

When King Philip of Spain died in 1560, his devastated wife wouldn't allow him to be buried, but had his coffin accompany her everywhere.

Csar Peter III of Russia was crowned 34 years after he died. His coffin was opened so that the crown could be put on his head.

Before the days of lipstick, women used to colour their lips red with *cochineal*, a paste made from crushed beetles.

The law system drawn up by the Roman emperor Draco made every crime a capital offence – one for which the criminal could be executed.

Victorians made keepsakes such as pictures and jewellery from the hair of their deceased loved ones.

The body of William the Conqueror was too big for his coffin, so two soldiers jumped up and down on him to try to squish him in. This broke his back and made his stomach explode.

In the Middle Ages, the boys who looked after dogs used for hunting had to sleep in the kennels with them.

In England, suicide used to be illegal. The punishment for trying to kill yourself was death.

> **Eighteenth-century toothpaste recipes included burnt bread and dragon's blood. It's not quite as gruesome as it sounds – dragon's blood was resin collected from a red plant.**

In medieval France, a cockerel that was found sitting on an egg (which only hens normally do) was found guilty of being a devil and was burned at the stake.

> **In 1808, Tommy Otter was hanged for killing his girlfriend. His body was left chained in a tree and a year later a pair of blue tits made a nest in his skull and reared eight chicks.**

Archeologists in Peru have found skeletons of victims who had been tied up and left to be eaten by vultures, perhaps as a sacrifice.

Young British Prime Minister William Pitt the Younger was advised to drink a bottle of port a day to cure his gout... and instead died from liver damage at the age of 46.

In the 1800s, Mongolian prisoners were fastened into a wooden box little larger than a coffin where they were left to die. Some were given food for years, but never allowed out.

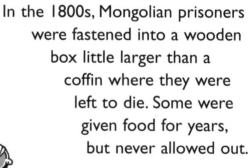

Houses in many parts of the world were built with wattle and daub – a mixture of horse manure and straw.

Horrible Science Facts

Albert Einstein's brain was removed, sliced up and preserved in jars by pathologist Dr Thomas Harvey. He kept it for 43 years before giving it to McMaster University, Ontario.

Faulty electrical wiring smells of rotten fish!

Burglars in Vienna fled when they found eight mummified heads in the basement flat they had broken into. The heads belonged to a dentist who was using them for research.

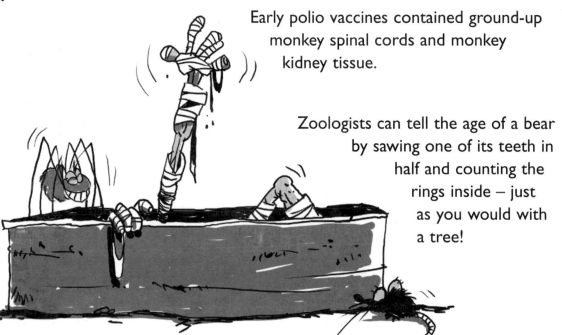

Early polio vaccines contained ground-up monkey spinal cords and monkey kidney tissue.

Zoologists can tell the age of a bear by sawing one of its teeth in half and counting the rings inside – just as you would with a tree!

The skull of a *Tyrannosaurus rex* was up to 1.5 metres (5 feet) long. Human-sized animals would still be alive while they were being munched in its mouth.

Australian rainbow plants look pretty, but in fact they are insect traps: the sticky leaves act as natural flypaper and glue the insects to the spot. The more they struggle, the more stuck they become.

It was 18th-century chemist Antoine Lavoisier who gave oxygen its name, but he ended up being deprived of it in a brutal way: he was beheaded during the French Revolution.

You can be struck by lightning even if you are indoors! A bolt can travel down phone lines, electric cables and plumbing pipes, so keep away from them during an electrical storm.

Castor bean extract *ricin* is twice as deadly as cobra venom. It was used on an umbrella tip to murder Bulgarian dissident Georgi Markov.

When photographic flashes are used, the eye's pupils cannot close fast enough, so the blood-rich retinas are illuminated. That's what gives people that devilish red-eye look in some pictures.

Stinkhorn mushrooms reek of dung! This is to attract flies, which then fly off with spores on their feet and spread them elsewhere.

Camels
are able to
completely seal
their nostrils to stop
sand going up
their noses.

If you knock your friends out with the smelly breath after eating garlic, it's down to your blood. The garlic pong travels in blood that supplies the lungs, transferring the smell to your breath.

A *chamois* is a type of goat. Lots of people polish their cars with chamois leathers – nice bits of goatskin.

Trans fats are man-made fats that are used for deep-frying and in processed foods. These nasty fats can lead to coronary heart disease by clogging up the body's arteries.

The smell made by rotten eggs, sewers and the worst farts is caused by a toxic, flammable gas called *hydrogen sulphide*.

Most people have grown all their wisdom teeth by the age of 30. The oldest person to grow a new tooth was 76.

The temperature of volcano lava can be as hot as 1200 degrees Celsius (2200 degrees Fahrenheit) – 12 times hotter than boiling water.

Ear infection *otitis* causes swelling and itching of the skin lining the ear canal. It can also make the ear produce a yucky, foul-smelling discharge.

Sea lice are gourmet guzzlers;
they feed on the mucus in fish gills.

Plastic surgeons sometimes
insert breast implants through
the belly button; it is cut open
and stretched, allowing the
surgeon to fit his whole arm
inside in order to put the implant
in place.

**Many food
thickeners are made
from *carageenan* and
gelatin – that's seaweed
and animal hooves
to you and me.**

The serious bacterial infection *salmonella*
is found in the faeces of some birds and reptiles,
so make sure you wash your hands
after holding your friend's pet iguana…

**American Dr Charles Arntzen is
researching ways of creating fruits that
contain vaccines against disease.
A diphtheria banana might sound gross
but it's still better than an injection!**

Hot tubs may look enticing, but they can harbour the bacteria that cause the pneumonia-like infection Legionnaire's Disease, which is spread through contaminated evaporated water.

Ten per cent of all horseshoe crabs die just from being upside down. They cannot get back on their legs if flipped onto their backs when washed ashore by rough seas.

In the US, most cases of rabies are caught not from dogs but from bat bites. If unvaccinated, people with rabies develop brain swelling and die within days.

Jelly fungus is a wibbly-wobbly mushroom. It tastes like soil but you can eat it if you want to.

A newborn elephant calf will snort to get rid of all the fluids in its trunk. Probably best to stand clear if you don't want to be showered with trunk gunk.

Tarantulas have claws at the end of their legs to grip their prey with.

A *bezoar* is a 'stone' (made of compacted hair or other material), found inside the intestines of some animals. People used to put one in a drink in the belief that it would neutralize any poison that was lurking there. It did no such thing, of course.

The first filter-tipped cigarettes contained asbestos. As if they weren't deadly enough already!

Tarantulas have irritating, barbed hairs on their backs called *urticating* hairs. Some can even fire these at predators.

Chemical engineers have developed a spray-on skin. The special goo is designed to cover soldiers' wounds in war zones and can last for up to two weeks in mud and other nasty germ-filled environments.

The ozone layer that we need to protect us from the sun's harmful rays is actually made up of a stinky, poisonous gas. Lucky for us it's so high up!

Indian Professor Syed Abdul Gafoor refused to bury his mother when she died. Instead, he had her body preserved in a glass case in his home until he died 20 years later and they were buried together. Not surprisingly, his wife had left him before then!

Octopuses have three hearts: two for pumping blood through the gills and one for pumping blood around the body.

Sewer workers need emergency breathing apparatus when working amongst slow-flowing sewage, as it gives off high levels of methane gas and eggy sulphide smells.

In 2000, a study into the cleanliness of seats on the London Underground showed that a row of seats contained the remains of six mice, two large rats and one previously unheard of fungus.

Threadworm eggs are so tiny that you can't see them. They float in the air and can shoot up your nose uninvited – then they enter your stomach and hatch into little worms.

The Amazon ant steals eggs from other ant colonies. It covers the newly hatched ants in smelly substances called *pheromones* that make them think they're in the right colony and act as slaves to their new master.

Air that contains more than 50 per cent oxygen is toxic – breathing it in will cause lung damage.

American inventor Thomas Edison electrocuted several animals in his research on electricity. In 1903, he filmed the death by electrocution of a zoo elephant that had killed three people and the film was seen by many people across the US.

After a skin injury, scar tissue growth can get out of control and form a big, rubbery lump called a *keloid*.

In 2006, a crowd control device was patented that shoots a stream of slime at troublemakers so that they slip and fall over, finding it impossible to get up again.

The skin infection *ringworm* is not caused by a worm but by a fungus (which is far preferable).

In hot, dry conditions, a dead body will naturally mummify instead of decomposing. The crew members of the American *Lady Be Good* military plane were found mummified 17 years after they crashed in the Libyan desert.

An emu has an inflatable neck sac that it uses to make strange noises – a bit like the funny sounds you can make when you let down a balloon.

Clarence Dally was an American researcher who worked on early X-rays. His habit of testing X-ray tubes on his own hands caused cancers so aggressive that his arms had to be amputated.

Oophagy is the eating of eggs in the womb by developing shark embryos. That's taking sibling rivalry a step too far!

Marine bloodworms have such pale skin that you can see their blood flowing underneath it.

After problems on re-entry, the crew of the Russian *Voskhod 2* spacecraft landed in the middle of the Ural Mountains. They spent a whole night surrounded by howling wolves before they were rescued.

Dogs will quite happily eat their own vomit.

Shark liver oil may sound foul, but it's bursting with vitamins and healing substances. It has been used by fisherman for centuries to soothe skin complaints and wounds.

Camels are cool customers; they begin to sweat only when the temperature goes above 41 degrees Celsius (106 degrees Fahrenheit). This saves them about five litres (10 pints) of water a day.

Mal de Débarquement Syndrome is seasickness without the sea. After being on a boat, sufferers still feel like they are in rough seas when they are back on land. Some can feel queasy for years afterwards.

The *Cobra Lily* plant looks like a rearing cobra, complete with leaves that resemble forked tongues. It has a gooey secretion and downward pointing hairs on its leaves to drag unsuspecting insects inside for food.

Butyric acid is what causes the acrid smell of rancid butter, Parmesan cheese and vomit.

If you use a sponge in the bath or shower, then you should think twice – it harbours more bacteria than the toilet bowl!

If you can face cooking pongy *stinkhorn* mushrooms, they taste of fish.

While on a plant-hunting expedition in Hawaii, 19th-century Scottish botanist David Douglas fell into a pit trap. A bull then fell on top of him and killed him.

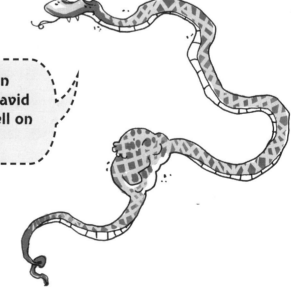

If ground temperatures are cold enough during a storm, rain can turn into ice as it falls. During the North American ice storm of 1998, many barns collapsed from the weight of the ice on their roofs, crushing the animals inside.

Most types of tarantula will eat each other, so if you're thinking of having one as a pet, don't get another one to keep it company.

The tongue of a blue whale is the size of an elephant.

Jellyfish have no bones, no cartilage, no heart, no blood, no eyes and no brain. But they can sting you!

Tar pits are natural tar pools that have been around for thousands of years. Because they're so old, they're full of the fossilized remains of animals that have come to a sticky end there.

Trypanophobia is the fear of medical procedures involving injections or hypodermic needles and affects around 10 per cent of American adults.

The giant squid's body contains high levels of *ammonium chloride*, so it tastes horrid to humans. Sperm whales love it, though.

The mother of all acnes is known as *acne fulminans*, meaning 'exploding eruptions'.

The pretty foxglove is also known as 'dead man's bells' and 'witches' gloves' as it is highly toxic, causing symptoms such as vomiting, delirium, convulsions and heart attacks.

The teeth of sharks are constantly being replaced. One shark can get through 30,000 teeth in its lifetime.

Pigs will eat any kind of faeces – their own, another animal's, human – they're not fussy!

Without the pull of normal gravity, body fluids move to the upper body. This means that astronauts in space have bulging neck veins, a swollen face and lots of nasal mucus.

The roots of the American *bloodroot* plant contain a toxic blood-red sap that causes lesions on the skin.

Scottish biologist Alexander Fleming was so messy that his laboratory was often littered with mouldy old dishes – that's how he discovered the antibiotic *penicillin*.

Potassium chloride is used to stop the heart during heart bypass surgery, when a pump is connected to the body to temporarily take over the job of the heart and lungs.

Salt stops the growth of bacteria and fungi, so was sometimes used to preserve dead bodies.

Deadly *hydrogen cyanide* gas smells of almonds... but 40 per cent of people cannot smell it.

Four square kilometres (about two and a half square miles) of land can contain up to a million worms.

Antiseptics killed more soldiers than diseases did during the First World War. They would destroy the body's natural defences and allow bacteria inside deep wounds to take over.

Doctors have been used as torturers throughout history. They know exactly where it hurts!

Viruses were purposely introduced in Australia to reduce the rabbit population. *Myxomatosis* gave the poor bunnies fatal tumours and *rabbit calicivirus* made them bleed to death.

Water and electricity are a deadly combination, as water conducts electricity. No one told poor Claude François, who was electrocuted when he tried to fix a light fitting whilst standing in a filled bath.

Bacteria have been around for billions of years, but some have recently become resistant to antibiotic drugs through gene mutation, creating apparently invincible superbugs.

Some sea spiders have six pairs of legs. That's some creepy-crawly.

Male elephants go through phases of madness. They become very aggressive and a tar-like substance is secreted from glands at the side of the head.

Ball lightning is the scariest form of lightning. A deadly ball of electricity hovers eerily in the air like a little spaceship, ready to strike.

Spider angiomas are harmless bumps on the surface of the skin. Made up of small blood vessels, they have a red spot in the middle with branches leading off, like a red spider's web.

The superbug MRSA can affect healthy people and kill them within four days. Don't think you can escape it in hospital, as that's the most likely place to pick it up!

Lying on your right side helps excess gas escape from the stomach more easily, so you can burp yourself to sleep.

In 1971, the crew of *Soyuz 11* space shuttle died after a broken valve allowed them to be exposed to the vacuum of space. Without air, their bodies would have exploded before they suffocated.

During the Second World War, American scientists planned to release bomb-carrying bats over Japan that would hide in buildings until the tiny bombs went off. The war ended before they finished their research so they never found out if it worked.

A *parasitic twin* is a foetus without a brain or internal organs that grows inside a normally developing twin. Kazakh boy Alamjan Nematilaev was seven years old before doctors realized he had the body of his twin inside him.

Rat-tailed maggots are hoverfly larvae. Their 'tail' is a kind of snorkel that can be as long as 15 centimetres (6 inches) and allows the maggot to breathe through it, if submerged.

The *gastrocolic reflex* is the name for what happens when you eat and your body decides you need to make room for the food by getting rid of some at the other end!

Cows can get *lumpyskin disease* if bitten by insects carrying the infection. (The clue to the symptoms is in the name.)

Sweat bees are attracted to the salt in human sweat and some are emerald green in colour. Don't worry, the sting hurts only a little bit.

At 28,000 degrees Celsius (50,432 degrees Fahrenheit) a lightning bolt is five times hotter than the surface of the sun.

Acid rain is caused by industrial gases like *sulphur dioxide*. In highly industrialized areas, the pH level of acid rain can be lower than 2.4 – more acidic than vinegar.

Bats' teeth are razor sharp so that they can chomp through hard insect shells.

It's important to drink enough water, but drinking too much can be dangerous. *Water intoxication* makes the brain swell and in severe cases will stop it functioning.

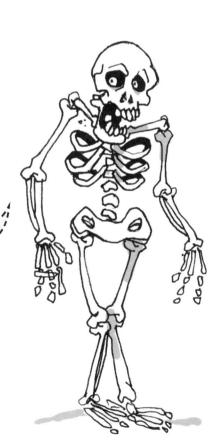

African honeybees are known as killer bees because they will swarm at the slightest provocation, entirely covering their victim.

Baboon spiders have large pads on the end of their legs that look like a baboon's feet.

Scientists have warned that our neighbouring galaxy, *Andromeda*, is heading for a collision with the *Milky Way* (our galaxy) in the distant future. If Earth is near the collision site, it will disappear in a less than a second. No one will feel a thing, though, so that's okay.

Tarantulas have eight eyes, but some species can't see a thing with them! They rely on their extreme sensitivity to vibrations and their sense of touch to catch their prey.

Ancient Greek physician Herophilos was the first to study the human body by dissecting it (opening it up). He did most of his studies on living people, but it was thought to be okay because they were only criminals.

The air pollution in Victorian London was so bad that the smelly fogs were nicknamed 'pea-soupers'.

When the liver stops working properly, the skin and the whites of the eyes turn yellow. Yellow fever got its name from these symptoms.

Russian scientist Alexander Bogdanov had many blood transfusions in the belief that they made him feel younger. In fact it was a blood transfusion that killed him, since the blood came from a student carrying malaria and tuberculosis.

Hairy wart and **foot rot** are infections affecting animals with hoofs.

Marine bloodworms grow up to 35 centimetres (about 14 inches) in length and have four jaws that are so strong they can cause agony if they bite!

The secretive Aghori tribe is so fearless of death that members live in graveyards, use human bones and ash in their rituals, and drink from human skulls.

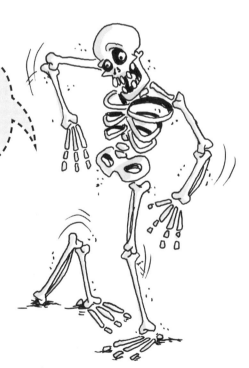

The *tarantula hawk* is a type of wasp with a stinger that is 7 millimetres (1/3 inch) long. The sting is as painful as you'd expect!

The venom of the Asian giant hornet is a nasty cocktail of chemicals: as well as a pain-causing substance, it contains an enzyme strong enough to dissolve skin and a scent to attract more hornets to the victim.

The world's deadliest tornado hit Bangladesh in 1989. It destroyed an area of 6 square kilometres (about 2.5 square miles) and killed 1,300 people.

When you cut an onion, the gas released reacts with the water in your eyes to produce a diluted form of *sulphuric acid*.

Vog is the toxic fog containing sulphur dioxide and other nasty gases that appears after a volcano eruption. Not only does it cause breathing problems, it stinks, too.

Hyalophagia is the eating of glass. Only mad people and circus performers do it.

Many 18th-century milkmaids were immune to the deadly smallpox infection. English doctor Edward Jenner linked this to their exposure to the pus in the blisters that appeared on their skin when they caught cowpox. It may have been nasty, but it protected them against smallpox.

An ostrich's eye is bigger than its brain. Have a look next time you see one but don't get too close – what it lacks in brains it makes up for in leg muscles.

In 1949, a monkey called Albert II became the first monkey to travel in space. Unfortunately, poor Albert died on impact when he returned from his mission.

A warning sign of an approaching tsunami is the sea receding dramatically, leaving fish flapping about on the sand. Resist the urge to have a look, just run!

Struggling in quicksand will give you that sinking feeling… the gloopy mixture contains a lot of water, so if a person relaxes it should help them to float and to be able to get out by using slow movements.

Some fungal skin infections glow in the dark.

Frogs, rats, wasps, and chicken embryos, fungi, have all been sent into space to research the effects of space flight on them. They weren't all in the same rocket though!

Elephants die when their teeth are worn down and they can't feed properly. They have five sets of teeth in their lifetime, but would live longer if they had more.

The leg bones of a bat are so thin that it can't walk on them. They would snap if it tried.

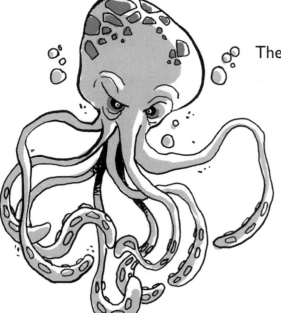

The pupil of an octopus's eye is rectangular.

Heartburn is caused by stomach acid being regurgitated into the oesophagus. The acid causes a burning sensation in the chest, throat and sometimes even the jaw.

Ever wondered why you want to vomit if you see someone else do it? Scientists believe this is a trait that evolved in ancient times; if one of a group foraging for food was sick, it was likely that they had all eaten something bad and had to get rid of it quickly.

Emu fat is a very good skin moisturiser. It won't make you run any faster, though.

Camel urine is thick and syrupy. Since camels often have to survive on little water, their kidneys are extremely efficient.

In his study on jellyfish, Dr Jack Barnes purposely stung himself and his 9-year-old son with the tiny but highly venomous *irukandji* jellyfish. All in the name of research!

Ants cannot chew their food. They have to chop away at it with their *mandibles* (jaws) that move sideways, like scissors.

The earliest transplant operation is said to have been performed in the 3rd century by twin saints Cosmas and Damian. They replaced the ulcerated leg of a patient with the healthy one of an Ethiopian. How successful it was is anybody's guess!

An explosion during an experiment left German chemist Robert Bunsen blinded in one eye by flying glass.

Lobsters and octopuses have blue blood. This is because the protein that transports oxygen round their bodies is rich in copper.

Giant tubeworms live in deep ocean seabeds and have no mouth or gut. They can be up to 3 metres (10 feet long) and live on a cocktail of chemicals spewed out of the earth that kills just about everything else.

Female dogs were used during Russian space flight experiments, as they did not need to lift their legs to urinate. No room for that in a space capsule!

It was 18th-century Italian scientist Luigi Galvani who discovered electrical impulses in nerves and muscles whilst doing experiments on static electricity. A static-loaded scalpel touched a dissected frog and its leg hopped into life!

Southern California is heading north! It is moving very slowly and will collide with Alaska in about 150 million years' time.

Sharks have no bones. Their skeletons are made of cartilage, which is lighter and more flexible.

If you fell into a black hole, you'd eventually come out again as light and bits of ash.

Bright colours on animals and insects warn predators that they taste yucky. The ladybird also secretes yellow, foul-smelling goo for any that haven't got the message!

Many tribes around the world have practised *trepanning* since the Stone Age. It involves drilling a hole in the skull, often with a stone, to ease headaches by letting out evil spirits. People frequently survived, as many skulls have been found with several such holes, some partially healed.

In 1962, a Dutch doctor decided to try trepanning. He used an electric drill to make a hole in his own head.

Early Indian surgeons used ants to hold the edges of wounds together. They would get an ant to bite through both sides of the wound, then twist off the ant's body and throw it away, leaving the head in place with the jaws acting as a stitch.

Malaria is a deadly disease spread by mosquitoes. It is caused by a tiny parasite that lives inside a person's blood cells. Malaria kills up to 1 million people a year.

If you fell into a black hole, you would be stretched into an incredibly long, thin string in a process called 'spaghettification'.

Railway workers in France in the 1800s claimed to have freed a Pterodactyl trapped in rock. They said it flapped, squawked and died. Reports of frogs and other animals trapped in solid rock are quite common, but not scientifically proven.

Snake venom is not normally poisonous if swallowed because stomach acid alters the chemicals in it.

A toxin in the nectar of laurels and rhododendrons causes the honey made from these plants to be poisonous. In 66 BC, Roman troops were lured by their enemies into a grove where bees made honey from these flowers. The soldiers ate it and were slaughtered while sick.

The scientific name for a fear of peanut butter sticking to the roof of your mouth is *arachibutyrophobia*.

One day you might be able to grow your own teeth to replace any bad ones. Scientists are researching growing new teeth in a laboratory using stem cells extracted from human milk teeth. Do you think it will put many dentists out of business?

Urine has been used for many things. In the past it was used as a cleaning fluid, thanks to its ammonia content, and also in the manufacture of gunpowder.

There are 'banks' where the umbilical cords of new babies can be stored in case future medical developments make it possible to grow new organs from the cells they contain.

Scientists investigating tumour growth added a gene from a firefly to make a glow-in-the-dark tumour. The tumour is visible through the skin of a test animal, so scientists can see if it grows or shrinks.

Some animals respond to small amounts of poisonous gas and have been used as early warning systems. German soldiers kept cats in the trenches of the First World War to smell gas, and British miners kept budgies in cages because they died quickly if gas escaped into the mine.

A fear of worms is called *scoleciphobia*.

There are over 20,000 road crashes involving kangaroos in Australia every year, so a robotic, kangaroo-like crash test dummy called Robo-Roo is used to test how badly cars will be damaged.

A person would need to weigh around 650 kilograms (1,433 pounds) to have enough fat to stop a bullet. Although their body would be bulletproof, they could still be killed by a shot to the head.

In 1999, an artist in Chicago, USA, announced his plan to create a glow-in-the-dark dog by adding a gene from jellyfish to it.

A third of the world's population is infected with tuberculosis (TB) – one person per second picks up the bacteria. Some people carry TB but do not become ill from it themselves.

Potatoes, aubergines, tomatoes and peppers all belong to the same family of plants as deadly nightshade!

Police scientists investigating a murder can work out how long a body has been dead by looking at the kinds of maggots, worms and insects that are eating it.

Scientists are working on a microscopic robotic tadpole to deliver medicines – the tadpole would 'swim' through the patient's blood vessels to take the medicine where it's needed.

Not all dead bodies rot. Under the right conditions, some of the fat can turn to a soap-like substance so that if the body is dug up, even years later, it can look much the same as when it was buried.

Palaeontologists find out about what dinosaurs ate by examining fossilized dinosaur faeces called *coprolites*. They have to be soaked in water for three days first to soften them.

An unusual form of drug abuse is licking cane toads. They make a slime containing a drug which produces hallucinations (strange experiences or visions). People in some parts of Australia and the USA have started licking the toads to enjoy the drug.

Fake mermaids made from bits of monkey and fish have been produced to fool scientists for years. One claimed to have been washed up by the tsunami in Asia in 2004. The oldest so-called mummified mermaid is 1,400 years old and is from Japan.

Australian Benjamin Drake Van Wissen invented machinery to mine *guano* (bird droppings) on the Pacific island of Nauru and turn it into fertilizer.

Green potatoes contain a poison, *solanin*, which can be deadly. It develops in old potatoes that are not kept in the dark. Eating 2 kilograms (4.4 pounds) of green potatoes could be fatal.

If you are trapped in snow in an avalanche, it's impossible to tell which way is up (and so which way to dig yourself out). Urinate and see which direction the yellow stain spreads – gravity will pull the urine down.

Oil is made from the decayed bodies of animals and plants that died millions of years ago and have been squashed deep underground.

There have been no cases of the deadly smallpox virus since 1978, but cultures of the virus are held at the Centers for Disease Control and Prevention in the United States and at the Institute of Virus Preparations in Siberia.

Since bats love to eat mosquitoes which cause malaria, an American scientist decided to use them to control the disease. He built bat roosts, towers specially designed to attract bats, near places infested with mosquitoes. After just a few years, the amount of malaria infection in these places dropped from 89 per cent to zero.

The most poisonous metal in the world is arsenic. It used to be made into flypaper for killing flies, but it killed some people, too.

If you cut spinach with an iron knife, both will turn black, as a chemical in the spinach reacts with the iron.

During the First World War, goldfish were used to check whether all traces of poisonous gas had been washed out of gas masks. The mask was rinsed and filled with water, then a goldfish was dropped in. If it died, there was still gas left in it.

Around 1,400 years ago, the Chinese used to make gunpowder by boiling up and burning pig manure. To make sure it was ready and not polluted with salt, they licked the crystals.

People used to use white lead powder to make their skin look white and beautiful, but it gave them lead poisoning and slowly killed them. As their skin looked worse once the poison took effect, they used more white lead to cover up the damage.

It can take 100 years for the body of a whale at the bottom of the sea to disappear completely, as it is slowly eaten away by different animals, plants and microbes.

Early matches were made of poisonous chemicals and would sometimes burst into flames on their own if they got warm and damp. They set fire to people's pockets unexpectedly! That must have been a bit of a shock!

A small animal such as a mouse can be dropped 1,000 metres (3,280 feet) down a mine shaft and suffer no harm because the fastest speed it can fall it is not enough to crush its body. The larger an animal or object, the shorter the distance it can safely fall.

Scraping mould off your food doesn't get rid of all of it – beneath the furry part, strings of mould can extend a long way down into the food itself.

Our blood is red because it uses an iron compound to carry oxygen – some spiders have blue blood because theirs uses a copper compound instead.

John Haigh killed six people in London, UK, in the 1940s, dissolving their bodies in a bath of acid, hoping he could wash away all the evidence. However, on finding three human gallstones and a pair of dentures belonging to one of his victims in the sludge left behind, the police had enough evidence to convict him.

Old cannonballs brought up from the seabed can explode and kill divers. Bacteria eat away part of the metal, producing gases that rapidly expand when the cannonballs come to the surface.

If you draw pictures in the condensation on a window, the picture will reappear the next time the window mists over as a layer of grease from your skin stays on the glass and repels the water.

Earthworms bring 4 million kilograms (8.8 million pounds) of earth to the surface per square kilometre (0.38 square mile) of open ground each year.

A medieval cure for stammering was scalding the tongue with a red-hot iron. It didn't work...

In the 1600s, spiders rolled in butter were recommended as a cure for malaria.

There have been several recorded cases of spontaneous human combustion (people who apparently burst into flames for no good reason). Sometimes, all that is left is a burnt patch and perhaps a foot or some singed clothing.

Rats trained to look for land mines are so light that they don't trigger the mechanism if they step on one. Instead, they scratch and bite at the ground when they smell explosives, and the handler deals with the mine.

Horses killed in the First World War were recycled as explosives – their fat was removed and boiled down to be used in making TNT.

If you fall off a very high cliff or building, the fastest speed you will ever fall is around 200 kilometres (124 miles) per hour. This is called terminal velocity, and it's enough to make a nasty splat.

Sleeping sickness is a fatal parasitic disease, but it can be treated. The only trouble is that the drug used to cure it contains arsenic and kills 10 per cent of patients who receive it.

Scientists believe that all *vertebrates* (animals with backbones) evolved from giant tadpoles, 6 centimetres (2.5 inches) long, that existed around 550 million years ago.

Some wealthy people have their bodies *cryopreserved* (deep frozen) when they die, in the hope that in the future, someone will find a cure for their cause of death and resurrect them. The popular urban legend that Walt Disney was cryopreserved is false – he was cremated.

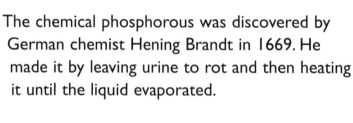

It is so cold in space, that urine flushed out of a space craft instantly freezes into a stream of yellow crystals.

A bolt of lightning is so incredibly hot that if it hits sand, it can turn it into glass!

The chemical phosphorous was discovered by German chemist Hening Brandt in 1669. He made it by leaving urine to rot and then heating it until the liquid evaporated.

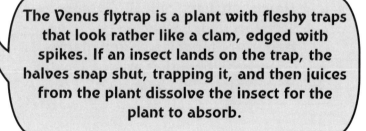

The Venus flytrap is a plant with fleshy traps that look rather like a clam, edged with spikes. If an insect lands on the trap, the halves snap shut, trapping it, and then juices from the plant dissolve the insect for the plant to absorb.

Lined up neatly, 10,000 bacteria would only stretch across your thumbnail.

A will-o'-the-wisp is a flame of burning marsh gas that appears in boggy areas at night. It has lured many travellers to a muddy death when they have left the path to follow it, believing it to be someone with a light.

The average bed is home to 6 million dust mites.

Japanese scientists have managed to grow tadpole eyes from scratch in the laboratory and transplant them into tadpoles. The eyes worked well even after the tadpoles changed into frogs.

In an emergency, coconut milk can be used as substitute for the watery part of blood in a blood transfusion.

Ergot is a fungus that grows on rye and causes people to act crazy if they eat it. Some historians think that people accused of witchcraft who said they could fly, or those who accused others of strange, magical behaviour, may have had ergot poisoning.

The germs present in faeces can pass through 10 layers of toilet paper – that's why you need to wash your hands!

The largest living thing in the world is a fungus in Washington state, USA, which covers 6 square kilometres (2.5 square miles) and has been growing for hundreds of years.

The Masai tribe in Africa drink cow or bull urine as a sedative (a drug to calm people down or make them sleepy).

There is a cockroach museum in Plano, Texas.

There are 100 million times more insects than people on Earth and their total weight is 12 times the total weight of the people.

Long before Scottish pharmacologist Alexander Fleming discovered penicillin, ancient Egyptians and ancient Greeks recognized that some moulds had antibacterial properties and used them for dressing wounds.

It's said that dead Americans rot much more slowly than they used to because the food they eat contains so many preservatives.

Some people – most of them in the USA – claim that they have been abducted by aliens from space while they slept, had their bodies experimented on and sometimes their minds changed, and were then returned to Earth.

Bacteria – tiny living things that we also call germs – divide in two every 20 minutes. So, starting with one (it doesn't need a girlfriend/boyfriend), you can have over 130 million in just 9 hours!

Some scientists think that being too clean might make us ill – some studies suggest that people need to eat a small amount of dirt in order to kick-start their immune systems. If our bodies do not learn to fight infections, it could lead to asthma and other allergic problems.

The average glass of London tap water has passed through nine people's bladders before it reaches your sink.

One possible way of controlling cockroaches being explored in the USA is to release parasitic worms which will kill the roaches but don't harm people.

The stinking corpse plant, or *rafflesia*, is a huge parasitic flower that smells like rotting meat. The flower is up to a metre (about 3 feet) across and is the largest flower in the world. It grows directly out of a creeping vine, from which it gains all its nourishment without ever growing leaves of its own.

Scientists working on transplant techniques grew a human ear on the back of a mouse. The ear was shaped by the human cartilage cells, but nourished as it grew by the mouse's blood.

Deodorants don't stop you sweating, but they kill the bacteria that make sweat smell.

The earliest study of brain damage was of railway worker Phineas Gage. In 1848, an explosion shot a thick iron rod through his head. Although he recovered physically, his character changed completely. His skull and the iron rod are on display at Harvard University, Boston, USA.

A Roman cure for epilepsy (having fits) was to bathe in the blood of a gladiator.

A cure for whooping cough used in Yorkshire, England, in the 1800s was to drink a bowl of soup with nine frogs hidden in it. You couldn't make it yourself – it only worked if you didn't know about the frogs. (And probably not then, either!)

Romans dressed small wounds with spiderwebs soaked in vinegar.

People on the Pacific island of Chuuk use a love potion made from centipede's teeth and stingray tails.

For centuries, it was illegal to cut up dead bodies, so surgeons and scientists had to pay criminals to steal the corpses of executed prisoners from the gallows in order to learn about anatomy.

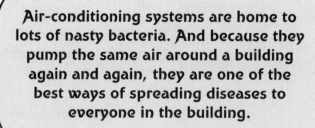

An old cure for tuberculosis consisted of cutting open a newly dead cow, pulling the folds of skin around your neck and breathing in deeply.

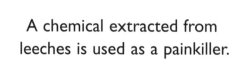

Air-conditioning systems are home to lots of nasty bacteria. And because they pump the same air around a building again and again, they are one of the best ways of spreading diseases to everyone in the building.

A chemical extracted from leeches is used as a painkiller.

Electric bug zappers splatter dead bugs around the room as they are vaporized by the lethal electric current.

A medieval cure for meningitis involved splitting a pigeon in two and laying the two halves, cut side down, on the patient's head.

The Australian 1991 Inventor of the Year Award was won by the designer of a cockroach zapper. The roach is lured into a trap with food, then electrocuted.

If you flush the toilet without putting the seat down, a fine aerosol spray of urine and faeces flies into the air of the bathroom, so some may land on your toothbrush.

A stinging tree in Australia can cause intense pain and even death. Tiny hairs full of poison break off the leaves and stick to the skin, which can then heal over the injury, trapping the poison inside. Even standing near the tree can cause painful nosebleeds!

An old cure for a headache involved tying the rope used to hang a criminal around your temples.

A common cure for all kinds of illnesses in the past was 'bleeding' the patient. This could be done by the doctor making a small cut and putting a hot cup over the wound to suck out blood, or by putting bloodsucking leeches on the skin. Using leeches is being reintroduced by some Western doctors.

In England in the 1500s, horse urine was rubbed into the scalp as a cure for baldness.

In the late 1800s, the Egyptian railways were fuelled by burning ancient mummies because they were more plentiful than coal and wood.

To catch the leeches for medical use, volunteers stand in rivers until the leeches attach themselves to their skin.

Australian performance artist Stelarc had a human ear grafted on to his forearm. He could literally turn a deaf ear to anyone who annoyed him.

A man who experimented with feeding a Venus flytrap – a type of flesh-eating plant – with bits of his own flesh found the plant could digest it easily. He used bits of his toes that had rotted and dropped off as a result of athlete's foot.

Sometimes frozen blocks of toilet waste flushed from aeroplanes fall to earth.

To investigate what owls eat, scientists take apart owl pellets (owl faeces) and piece together the bones and fur from different creatures the owl has eaten.

One of the best ways of cleaning an infected wound, used before the days of antibiotics and now with infections that antibiotics can't treat, is to put maggots into it to eat the rotting flesh.

Sundew plants have lots of sticky tentacles. When an insect lands on them, it can't escape and the glue on the plant digests the insect's body, feeding the plant.

In 1986, 92 people were killed in Bangladesh by giant hailstones weighing up to 1 kilogram (2 pounds 3 ounces) each.

The English rhyme *Ring-a-Ring-o'-Roses* dates from the time of the bubonic plague. The 'roses' refer to the red spots that appeared before the boils, the 'posies' to the flowers people carried around to counteract the bad air that they thought caused plague. Sneezing was an early symptom.

Scientists are working on a design for a spacecraft that will be partly fuelled by burning astronauts' faeces.

In the Middle Ages, people thought they could cure the medical condition *rheumatism* by carrying a dead shrew in their pockets.

The Fore people of Papua New Guinea traditionally eat the bodies of their dead relatives, including the brain. During the 1950s to 1960s an outbreak of the disease *kuru* was traced to the practice and people were dissuaded from enjoying the usual funeral meal.

The scientific name for fear of slime is *blennophobia*.

Some babies are born still enclosed in the sac that holds the fluid in which they develop in the womb. It used to be considered a sign of good luck. Second World War leader Winston Churchill was born like this.

Taking a bath in the water used to wash a corpse was thought to cure epilepsy.

In the 19th century, arsenic was often used to create green colouring. A cake with green icing, coloured with arsenic, killed children who ate it at a birthday party, prompting chemists to demand laws regulating what could be used in foods.

A new design for a rat trap sends a text message to a pest controller when it kills a rat, so that the rat can be quickly removed before it starts to decompose and smell.

Sometimes fish or frogs fall from the sky like rain and there have been cases of a shower of meat (lumps of lung and muscle) and a rain of maggots.

Plants aren't as harmless as they seem. There are more than 600 types of carnivorous plants, those that eat animals or insects.

Mucus is all stringy and stretchy as it has a mesh framework, a bit like a 3D version of a spider's web.

There are approximately 4,000 microbes lurking above every 6.4 square centimetres (1 square inch) of ground.

Bodies buried in lead-lined coffins sometimes explode, as gases from the rotting body are held in by the strong metal. If they are dug up and opened, bits of body can fly out in all directions.

Equipment retrieved from the moon in the 1970s contained germs left there in 1967 – they were still alive.

The strangler fig grows from a seed dropped into a crevice on another tree in bird or opossum faeces. The fig's roots grow down and around the host tree and eventually strangle the host tree to death.

Pitcher plants have a deep funnel filled with acid that dissolves any insects or small animals that fall into it. The dead creatures are used as food by the plant.

A zookeeper in Germany tried to treat an elephant for constipation with laxative foods and an enema (pumping oil into its anus through a tube). His cure was effective – the elephant produced 90 kilograms (200 pounds) of faeces, which landed on the keeper and suffocated him.

A firestorm is an uncontrollable fire, often the result of a bombing raid. Temperatures can rise to 800 degrees Celsius (1,472 degrees Fahrenheit) and air is sucked into the firestorm with the force of a hurricane. People who aren't burned can suffocate.

Fat contains a huge amount of energy. Polar explorers sometimes eat hunks of greasy seal fat to give themselves enough calories to keep their bodies warm.

The Great Book of Horrible Facts

Scabs are formed when chemical proteins react with special blood cells called platelets, which cause the blood to get sticky and clump together. Once the blood has clotted, lots of different chemicals and cells work together to dry out the clot and form a scab, keeping out germs while the cells underneath repair themselves. So, if you pick a scab, you're messing with all your body's hard work!

A French cement factory uses soiled nappies as fuel to heat its cement kilns.

In 1890, a young girl was smeared with *phosphorous* so that she would glow in the dark and could act as a ghost in a hoax séance. She was poisoned by the chemical and died.

Piles of horse manure steam in cold weather because the action of bacteria breaking it down produces so much heat. The manure, filled with water and gas, is a good insulator, so it stays hot.

In 2000, UK mountaineer Major Michael Lane gave a museum five of his own fingers and eight of his toes, which had dropped off as a result of frostbite when he was climbing Mount Everest in 1976.

Volcanic vents deep under the sea are home to strange plants and animals that can live in high temperatures and poisonous, acidic water.

It is possible to drown in mud – and almost impossible to save someone who is drowning in mud, as so much force is needed to pull them out.

Scientists studying Mormon crickets cut the heads off to see what the crickets had been eating – and found many had eaten other Mormon crickets. If one stopped to eat, another would often come along and eat it.

Doctors used to test for diabetes by tasting the patient's urine. It tasted sweet, since diabetes makes urine contain an excessive amount of sugar.

The first frozen chicken was created by Sir Francis Bacon, who stuffed a plucked chicken with snow in 1626 to experiment with refrigeration. It worked, but he died from a chill contracted during the experiment. The chicken is said to haunt Pond Square in London.

If blue whales tried to live on land, they would be crushed and suffocated by their own weight. They can live successfully in water because it supports them.

Scientists have created rice that contains human genes! Genetically modified rice was developed with a human liver gene and, more recently, saliva and breast milk proteins.

Diamonds are so hard that they are often used as the tip of a dentist's drill because they can grind through teeth.

On the east coast of the USA there is a laboratory that leaves dead bodies of humans and animals outside to decay so that scientists can study the rate at which they rot, and the maggots and microbes that help them decompose.

Honey kills germs. Spreading it on wounds can stop them from becoming infected.

Hungry huskies and polar bears have been known to attack explorers when they urinate – they are attracted by the smell.

Soap can be made by dissolving animal fat using an alkali such as *sodium hydroxide*. Soap used to be made from sheep or pig fat.

> Scientists have modified cockroaches, implanting electrodes in them to control their legs, and used them as living robots to carry cameras or explosives through tiny spaces.

Most bacteria are only about 0.00025 of a centimetre (0.0001 of an inch) across. But monster bacteria have been found at the bottom of the ocean off the coast of Africa. These bacteria are so big that they can be seen without a microscope – each one is about the size of the full stop at the end of this sentence.

Dermestid beetles are so good at stripping the flesh off dead animals that natural history museums use their larvae to clean up skeletons they are going to put on display.

Some types of pitcher plant have long trailing stems which capture and digest small animals such as frogs.

Scientists have tried running cars and tractors on chicken faeces! It's just one solution for the fuel shortage that will happen when oil and petrol run out.

Occasionally, babies are born with a full set of teeth.

In Chile, trains on the Arica-La Paz railway were at one time powered by burning llama faeces.

Horrible World Record Facts

CAUTION! Some of these World Record Facts are highly dangerous. They have been set by people who have trained for a long time and received strict medical guidance. Don't try any of them at home!

The largest foreign object left in a patient was a pair of 33 centimetre (13 inch)-long forceps, sewn inside Indian woman Meena Purohit after a Caesarean birth. The implement was discovered only when she had another operation four years later!

Robert Mark Burns peeled and ate a lemon in 46.53 seconds. He was sour-faced for hours afterwards.

Australian Stuart Ross ate 15 fiery-hot jalapeño chilli peppers in one minute.

Welshman Captain Beany from Planet Beanus (real name Barry Kirk) holds the unofficial world record for sitting in a bath full of gloopy, cold baked beans. He sat in it for 100 hours in 1986.

The heaviest marine crustacean is the American lobster. One caught in 1977 weighed over 20 kilograms (44 pounds). The lobster doesn't chew food in its mouth, it has teeth in its stomach to do that.

The biggest underpants in the world, bearing the slogan 'Pants to Poverty', measured 14.4 metres (47 feet 3 inches) wide. Let's hope they were clean.

American Lee Redmond's hideously long, curved nails have a total length of 7.51 metres (24 feet 7 inches). How does she go to the bathroom? Carefully!

An Arctic-dwelling whale known as a *narwhal* has a single enormous tusk. The tusk can grow to a length of 3 metres (9 feet 10 inches), which makes it the longest whale tooth.

The world's hairiest man is Yu Zhenhuan from China – his body is 96 per cent covered in long hair!

The elephant seal has a kind of trunk that it uses to make scary roaring noises. It can hold its breath for more than **80** minutes, which is longer than any other non-ocean-dwelling mammal.

Neolithic bodies found in Pakistan reveal man's earliest attempts at dentistry. Some of the 9,000-year-old skeletons discovered there had drilled and capped teeth. Open wide!

British man Gordon Mattinson can make his face look so gruesome that he has won the **World Gurning Championships** 10 times.

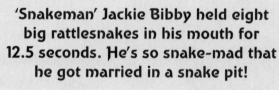

'Snakeman' Jackie Bibby held eight big rattlesnakes in his mouth for 12.5 seconds. He's so snake-mad that he got married in a snake pit!

The highest number of cows killed by lightning was **68** Jerseys that were sheltering under a tree, struck during a storm in Australia.

> Female *Queen Alexandra's birdwing* butterflies from Papua New Guinea are the biggest in the world and can have a wingspan of 30 centimetres (12 inches). Locals use blowguns to kill the rare butterflies so they can sell them to collectors.

The North Pacific Gyre is a huge vortex of slow, clockwise-revolving ocean water. It has drawn so much litter and waste into its centre that it is the largest ocean landfill site. It's known as The Great Pacific Garbage Patch!

> Before sensible boxing rules were introduced, Jack Jones and Patsy Tunney beat each other to a pulp in a fight that had 276 rounds and lasted 4 hours 30 minutes.

The water in the largest hot spring in Deildartunguhver, Iceland, is close to boiling point – so unless you want to make human soup, stay away!

A British man survived 90 per cent burns after an exploding canister covered him in petrol while he was filling his moped in 1996.

The longest cuddle ever lasted for 5,000 years! Archaeologists discovered a pair of entwined skeletons in Northern Italy and believe the couple to be from the Neolithic period.

Desert locusts have been the most destructive insects on the planet for thousands of years. A day's food for a regular swarm of 50 million locusts would feed 500 people for a whole year.

The first hairy earwig sanctuary was created in the 1960s in Sarawak, northern Borneo.

American Benjamin Drucker had 745 surgical needles stuck into his body in 2 hours 21 minutes to become the world record holder for the most piercings with 18-gauge surgical needles.

With his swollen gums, missing teeth, bald patches and overgrown claws, Chi-Chi the African sand dog has won the World's Ugliest Dog Contest seven times.

The most dangerous sea urchin is the *flower sea urchin*. Brushing against its toxic spines will cause severe pain, breathing problems and paralysis.

The *Ongaonga tree nettle* in New Zealand has the most dangerous plant sting. Brushing against it causes a sting that lasts for days. Falling into it can be fatal.

Sandeep Kaur's face and scalp were ripped off in one piece when her pigtails got caught in a threshing machine as a child. She had the first ever full-face transplant operation and went on to become a nurse.

The Black Sea is the largest *meromictic basin*. This means that it has deadly hydrogen sulphide gas trapped in its depths that could be released if there were an earthquake.

American stuntman Ted Batchelor's body was on fire for 2 minutes 36 seconds during a fire stunt in 2004, making it the longest full-body burn.

African Johannes Relleke was attacked by bees in 1962 and had the most number of bee stings ever removed: 2,443!

Indian man Radhakant Bajpai has the longest ear hair in the world, measuring 13.2 centimetres (5.19 inches). He believes it's a gift from God.

The largest toxic cloud, containing cancer-causing *beryllium*, covered an area of 300 kilometres (186 miles) and came from a 1990 factory fire in Kazakhstan.

Australian Grant Denyer was kissed by 62 people in one minute. That's 62 lots of bacteria-ridden saliva!

The world's most used method of execution is death by firing squad.

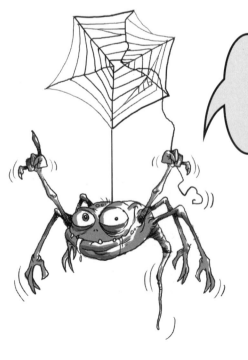

When is a worm not a worm? When it's the world's smallest snake, the *thread snake*. It looks like a worm, but if you look closely you can see its snaky eyes. It won't see you, as it's blind!

Ian Sharman ran the London marathon in 2007… dressed as Elvis! He broke the world record for the fastest man to run as Elvis, finishing in 2 hours and 57 minutes.

> **The largest animals to be gobbled up by big, carnivorous _pitcher plants_ are rats, frogs and lizards.**

The _thresher shark_ has the longest fin, with its tail fin being as long as the body and head. It's also known as a _swiveltail_, since it uses the huge fin to whack its prey unconscious before devouring it.

Human extinguisher Antti Karvinen put out 36 fire torches with his mouth in one minute in 2000.

Carbon dioxide-filled Lake Nyos in West Africa is the world's deadliest lake. Sudden eruptions release the gas without warning, suffocating animals and people nearby.

The record for sharing a coffin with the most cockroaches is held by 'Jungle' John LaMedica. He lay in a transparent coffin and had 20,050 giant Madagascan hissing cockroaches poured on top of him!

The great white shark is the largest predatory fish and can be as long as 6 metres (20 feet). Humans are generally too bony for it to eat, but it will still take a bite!

The world's most pierced man, Luis Antonio Agüero, has more than 175 ring piercings in his face alone. He has 55 more piercings in other parts of his body!

The ferocious *wolverine* is the largest land-dwelling weasel. It's also known as the *skunk bear*, as it will give off a nasty smell if annoyed.

The floppy nose of an old male *proboscis* monkey can be as long as 17.5 centimetres (7 inches) and hangs over its mouth.

The hairiest frog is… the hairy frog! The male adult frogs develop hairy thighs during the breeding season.

American Cathie Jung has deformed her body in the way Victorians used to. She has the narrowest corseted waist measurement of just 38 centimetres (15 inches).

The Venus flytrap plant can snap its leaves shut around a juicy insect in just one tenth of a second.

British performer Scott Bell didn't get cold feet for his record attempt. He walked 76.2 metres (250 feet) over burning hot embers.

The fish with the most eyes is the six-eyed *Pacific spookfish*.

The worst firework disaster killed around 800 people in Paris during royal wedding celebrations in 1770. Firework sparks ignited other fireworks prematurely, starting a fire and causing the crowds to stampede.

At 32 centimetres (13 inches) tall, the African goliath frog is the largest frog on earth. It can jump 3 metres (10 feet) in one go, but can only do this a couple of times before it needs a rest.

The ocean sunfish is the heaviest bony fish and can weigh up to 2 tonnes (4,400 pounds). It looks like the ugliest, too – it has one bulging eye, it can't close its mouth and its toxic, sandpapery skin is covered in mucus.

The vicious honey badger is the most fearless mammal: it can kill and eat a snake measuring 150 centimetres (5 feet) in 15 minutes and can take hundreds of bee stings too!

Palaeontologists discovered the stalest vomit ever in Peterborough, England, in 2002: 160 million-year-old fossilized vomit from a marine reptile.

The largest fish egg ever discovered was that of a whale shark in 1953. It was more than 30 centimetres (1 foot) long and had a live embryo wriggling around inside it!

The heart of a blue whale is the largest of any animal. The aorta is 23 centimetres (9 inches) wide and the heart itself is the size of a small car. Plenty of room for a family of four.

The sport of haggis hurling involves throwing a haggis as far as is humanly possible. The furthest distance so far is 55.11 metres (180 feet 10 inches).

The
World Ball Cup
is a testicle-cooking
competition held
annually in Serbia. Teams
of chefs cook bull,
boar and camel
testicles.

Louise Hollis has been growing her toenails since 1982 and the combined length of all ten nails is over 2 metres (over 7 feet). She may not be able to wear shoes or walk properly, but at least she's a world record holder!

Park ranger Roy C Sullivan survived being struck by lightning. Not once, not twice, but seven times.

The largest feline carnivore, the Siberian tiger, can munch 45 kilograms (100 pounds) of meat in one go. It can eat a bear but luckily it isn't too interested in munching on people.

Attention-seeker Jerome Abramovitch inflates his forehead and cheeks by injecting saline into them, creating a disfigured 'Elephant Man' look.

Canadian ginger tabby cat Jake has 28 toes – 7 on each paw!

At the World Mosquito Killing Championships in 1995, Henri Pellonpaa killed 21 mosquitoes in 5 minutes... using just his hand!

People desperate for tickets to see the 2006 Filipino game show *Wowowee* stampeded, causing the most game show deaths (74 people were trampled to death).

Bombay blood (h-h) is such a rare blood group that anyone needing an urgent blood transfusion of that type would be highly unlikely to get it, and would most likely die.

The largest garlic festival in Gilroy, California, lasts three days. Garlic ice cream, anyone?

Russian dog Laika was the first dog to enter Earth's orbit, but she was not meant to return. Her food for the tenth day contained fatal poison, but faulty temperature controls meant that she died from heat exhaustion a few hours after take-off anyway.

Some 13,000-year-old skeletons discovered in caves in Indonesia were found to be from a race of little people that were just a metre (3 feet 3 inches) tall.

The most toxic man-made chemical, known as TCDD, is 150,000 times more deadly than cyanide. Just what the world needs!

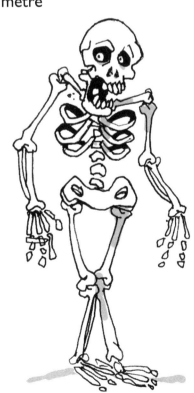

Monster saltwater crocodiles killed 9,980 Japanese soldiers who tried to cross Burmese mangrove swamps in 1945, making it the worst crocodile attack ever.

US park ranger Roy Sullivan was hit by lightning a record seven times during his career working in Shenandoah National Park in Virginia. He survived them all and became known as the 'Human Lightning Conductor'.

The deadliest natural toxin doesn't come from any plant or animal but from bad food. *Clostridium botulinum* is more poisonous than arsenic or snake venom and causes the deadly illness *botulism*.

Australian Andrew Hajinikitas drank 120 millilitres (4.2 fluid ounces) of tongue-obliterating Tabasco Sauce in 30 seconds.

The most expensive food is black, smelly fish eggs: Almas caviar is worth £20,000 ($32,000) per kilogram.

The worst lightning strike disaster killed 81 people when a Boeing 707 jet was struck in 1963.

Croatian police seized 10 mobile phones in 2000. The phones were cleverly disguised pistols that could fire deadly bullets if the number 5678 was dialled.

The most expensive bar of soap ever made supposedly contained fat taken from Italian Prime Minister Silvio Berlusconi during liposuction. It cost £10,000 ($16,000).

Argentinians eat the most beef – they get through over 2 million tonnes (4 billion pounds) a year!

American Rob Williams made a ham, cheese and lettuce sandwich using his feet in 1 minute 57 seconds.

The world's oldest piece of cake was found in an Ancient Egyptian tomb and is 4,200 years old!

The biggest Japanese spider crab ever found had a leg span of 3.69 metres (12 feet 1 inches). These monsters can live for 100 years.

Bobby Leach was the first man to go over Niagara Falls in a barrel, surviving his multiple injuries. He went out with less of a fanfare, dying from gangrene after slipping on some orange peel.

Canadian Aaron Gregg juggled three running chainsaws and made 86 catches. Some people would give their right arm to do that!

Irishman Vincent Pilkington killed and plucked 100 turkeys in 7 hours and 32 minutes in 1978.

Canadian Christopher Tyler Ing had a nipple hair that was 8.89 centimetres (3.5 inches) long.

The liver is the largest internal organ and can be up to 22 centimetres (8.6 inches) long. If it's not working properly, just one of the things that can happen is that your fingernails drop off.

The most polluted town is Dzerzhinsk in Russia, where life expectancy for a man is 42 years. The town is full of factories producing chlorine, pesticides and chemical weapons.

The Peregrine falcon is the fastest creature on earth. It can knock out a smaller bird with a single blow and will break the bird's neck if it hasn't died on impact. Then the falcon will use its sharp beak and talons to rip the prey apart and eat it!

Large, biting *tsetse flies* are the least picky bloodsuckers of vertebrates. They'll bite anything that has a backbone – they're not fussy!

The largest insect swarm ever was made up of 10 billion locusts that invaded Kenya in 1954.

Male African cicadas produce the loudest insect sound. By vibrating their special membranes, their call can reach 106 decibels!

The longest millipede ever discovered was 38.7 centimetres (15.2 inches) long and had 256 legs!

Japanese *macaques* are the northernmost population of non-human primates. Their faces, hands and bottoms are bright red!

The largest burrowing animal is the Australian wombat. Small wombats may look cute, but a fully-grown one can charge at a man, knock him over and leave a 2 centimetre (1 inch) deep bite in his leg!

Anaconda snakes have the biggest difference between the sexes amongst vertebrates: the females are five times bigger than the males.

The largest land carnivore is the polar bear, which spends the whole winter feasting on seals. It can also manage a huge walrus and even a beluga whale.

Indian boy Devendra Harne has 12 fingers and 13 toes.

The most expensive soup is made with shark's fin, sea cucumbers and other yucky (and illegal) stuff. *Buddha-jumps-over-the-wall* soup over £100 a bowl and has to be ordered five days in advance.

The brain removed from an American man in 1992 weighed 2.3 kilograms (5 pounds 1 ounce); almost twice as much as an average one. He certainly had more brains than most!

Traces of smallpox have been found in Egyptian mummies 3,000 years old. In Europe, by the 18th century, the disease was killing around 400,000 people a year.

Alan 'Nasty' Nash crushed 23 eggs with his toes in 30 seconds. Cheese omelette, anyone?

The USA has the largest death row population in the world, with more than 3,000 prisoners awaiting execution.

The *peacock mantis* shrimp has the fastest recorded 'punch' of any animal! Its front leg moves at 23 metres (75 feet) per second to club its prey. It keeps punching the shell of its prey mercilessly, until it makes a hole through which it can feed. Seconds away, round one!

The deadliest magic trick is the bullet-catching trick. At least 11 people have died whilst performing it.

The largest cat is a *liger* – a lion mates with a tigress and the hybrid offspring grows up to be twice as big. Imagine if you grew up to be twice as tall as your dad!

The parasite that affects the most humans is also the most fertile – a female roundworm can produce 26 million eggs in her lifetime. She must die of exhaustion!

The gaboon viper has the longest fangs of any snake. It delivers a venom so toxic that the affected body part often has to be amputated.

Nepenthes albomarginata is the fussiest insect-eating plant – it will only eat termites! A hungry plant will lure 22 termites a minute into its tubular leaves.

'Rubber boy' Daniel Browning Smith can dislocate his arms and legs to squeeze through a tennis racket-sized hole in 15 seconds!

Peter Dowdeswell ate 4.5 kilograms (12 pounds) of ice cream in 45.5 seconds. Then he had the mother of all brain freezes.

Bert is the reserve Deputy Sheriff for the Los Angeles County Sheriff's Department. He might kick you if you break the law, but that's because he's a camel.

The lava that comes from the Ol Doinyo Lengai volcano in Tanzania is the coldest in the world... but it's still 600 degrees Celsius (1,112 degrees Fahrenheit).

Charles Osbourne, from Iowa, USA, hiccupped every 1.5 seconds for 69 years and then suddenly stopped.

The most expensive coffee in the world is made with coffee beans recovered from the faeces of the civet, a type of wild cat from Sumatra.

At a single meal, obese New Yorker Walter Hudson could eat: 12 doughnuts, 10 packets of crisps, 8 Chinese take-aways and half a cake!

Gary 'Stretch' Turner holds the the world record for the planet's stretchiest skin. He suffers from Ehlers-Danlos syndrome, a condition which has left his skin so thin that he can pull his neck skin up over his mouth.

Peter Dowdeswell of the UK ate a three-course meal in a record 45 seconds in 1999. He ate oxtail soup, mashed potatoes, baked beans and sausage, and then prunes.

Natasha Verushka of the USA holds the record for sword swallowing. At a convention in 2004 she swallowed 13 swords.

> The biggest cockroach in the world is the Madagascan hissing cockroach. It can grow to 9 centimetres (3.5 inches) – as long as an adult's finger.

Monte Pierce of the USA can flick a coin 3.3 metres (10 feet 10 inches) with his earlobes.

The black-headed sea snake found north of Australia in the Timor Sea is 100 times more deadly than the most poisonous snake on land.

Leonardo d'Andrea from Italy smashed 32 watermelons with his head in 1 minute in 2005.

Kevin Cole from the USA shot a strand of spaghetti out of his nose a distance of 19 centimetres (7.5 inches) in 1998.

Frenchman Marc Quinquandon set a world record by eating 144 snails in 11 minutes. He beat his own record when he ate 72 snails in 3 minutes, but he died soon afterwards.

In 2005, Matthew Henshaw from Australia swallowed a sword 40.5 centimetres (15.9 inches) long, and hung a sack of potatoes weighing 20 kilograms (44 pounds 5 ounces) on its handle for 5 seconds.

The biggest beetle in the world is the dung-eating Goliath beetle – it's about the size of a hamster!

In 1998, 13 year-old Daniel Canal of Florida, USA, received 12 transplanted organs in only 3 weeks.

The loudest recorded scream was 129 decibels, made by Jill Drake of the UK at a Halloween celebration in 2000.

By March 2005, American Donald Gorske had eaten 20,500 Big Macs. He has eaten at least one a day for 33 years.

Gordon Cates of the USA holds the record for kissing poisonous snakes. He kissed 11 cobras in 1999.

A woman who worked on smelly feet in a testing laboratory had to smell 5,600 feet over 15 years.

A Japanese woman holds the record for having the most worms removed from her stomach – doctors removed a total of 56 in 1990.

Tom Shufflebottham charmed 511 worms out of the ground at a worm-charming championship in England in 1980.

Norman Gary of the USA held 109 live honeybees in his mouth for 10 seconds in 1998.

The world's most premature surviving baby was Amillia Taylor, who was just the length of a ballpoint pen when she was born at less than 22 weeks.

Danny Capps holds the record for spitting a dead cricket out of his mouth, reaching a distance of 9.17 metres (30 feet).

Michael Lloyd of the USA holds the record for kicking himself in the head – 42 times in a row!

Hu Saelao of Thailand has not cut his hair for more than 70 years.

The two smelliest substances are gross gases that the US government is investigating as possible weapons. They would be used to break up crowds without harming people. One is called Who Me? and the other is called The US Government Standard Bathroom Malodor.

Ken Edwards of the UK ate 36 live cockroaches in one minute on a breakfast TV show in 2001.

Ciro Gallo of the UK holds the record for having concrete blocks broken on his chest with a sledgehammer, while lying on a bed of nails – 37 blocks weighing a total of 235.8 kilograms (519.8 pounds).

In 1999, American Scott Jeckel shot a marshmallow 4.96 metres (16.27 feet) out of his nose, with his friend Ray Perisin catching it in his mouth.

The longest-lasting operation took 96 hours and was carried out in Chicago, USA, in 1951 to remove a giant tumour.

Dustin Phillips of the USA can drink a whole bottle of tomato ketchup through a straw in only 33 seconds.

Shridhar Chillal grew his fingernails for 44 years without cutting them. Their average length was 117 centimetres (46 inches), and his thumbnail was 132 centimetres (52 inches).

Robert Earl Hughes of Illinois, USA had the largest chest measurement ever recorded. He was 3.15 metres (10 feet 4 inches) around the chest when he died, aged 32. He weighed 484 kilograms (1,067 pounds).

In 1976, American Jon Brower Minoch weighed 635 kilograms (1,400 pounds). He was so fat that it took 12 firemen to lift him out of his house when he fell ill, and 13 nurses to turn him over in bed. In fact, he had two beds strapped together as one wasn't big enough to hold him. He once put on 89 kilograms (196 pounds) in a single week.

The smallest fully grown adult ever to live was Gul Mohammed of India, who was 57 centimetres (34.5 inches) tall at the age of 33 and weighed only 17 kilograms (37.5 pounds).

The record for spitting a mouthful of tobacco is 16.23 metres (53 feet 3 inches), set in 1997.

The longest recorded eyebrow hair was 7.8 centimetres (3.1 inches) long.

The worst epidemic of all time was the Black Death – a plague carried by fleas that live on rats. It killed some 75 million people in Europe and Asia between 1347 and 1351.

The most poisonous fish in the world is the stonefish. Stepping on its spines causes a painful death in 20 minutes.

A hair ball weighing 2.53 kilograms (5 pounds 3 ounces) was removed from the stomach of a 20-year-old English woman in 1895.

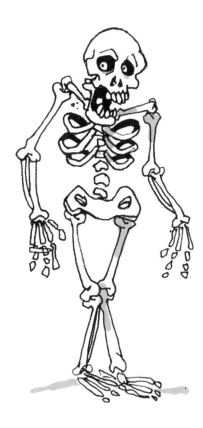

The largest-ever kidney stone – a solid mass of mineral that collects inside the kidneys – weighed 356 grams (12.5 ounces). It was removed from a man in Australia in 2003.

The longest leg hair grew on Australian Tim Stinton – it was 12.4 centimetres (4.9 inches) long.

The winner of a fly-swatting contest in 1912 killed 543,360 flies, weighing a total of 96 kilograms (212 pounds).

Kim Goodman from the USA can 'pop' her eyeballs out of their sockets so that they stick out 11 millimetres (0.4 inches).

Motorcycle stunt rider Evel Knievel of Montana, USA, holds the record for suffering the most broken bones — he suffered 435 fractures while working as a stuntman before he died in 2007.

A man in Bulgaria who accidentally shot himself in 1942 still has the bullet lodged in his head.

Thomas Wedders, who lived in England in the 1770s, is said to have had a nose that was 19 centimetres (7.5 inches) long.

The youngest person to have a full set of false teeth was only 4 years old. He suffered from an inherited disease that destroyed his teeth.

American Robert Wadlow had the largest feet ever recorded. They were 47 centimetres (18.5 inches) long.

The longest word in the English language is supposedly the name of a lung disease called *pneumonoultramicroscopicsilicovolcano-coniosis* – some experts say it is not actually a valid word at all.

Monte Pierce from the USA can stretch his left earlobe to a length of 12.7 centimetres (5 inches).

Stephen Taylor from the UK can stick his tongue out 9.4 centimetres (3.7 inches) measured from the tip to his lips.

The longest beard ever was grown by Hans Langseth of Norway, whose whiskers stretched an incredible 5.33 metres (17.6 feet) when measured at his death in Kensett, Iowa, in 1927. The beard was presented to the Smithsonian Institution, in Washington DC, in 1967.

Giovanni Batista from Orsenigo, Italy, has a collection of more than 2 million human teeth.

Sarwan Singh, who lives in Canada, has the longest beard on a living man. In 2010 it was 2.37 metres (7 feet 9 inches) long.

Thomas Blackthorne of the UK can lift 11 kilograms (24 pounds) of weights using just his tongue.

Rene Alvarenga of El Salvador has eaten 35,000 live scorpions. He catches them himself with his bare hands and eats 20 to 30 per day.

Garry Turner of the UK once clipped 159 wooden clothes pegs to his face at the same time.

Frenchman Michel Lotito is called Monsieur Mangetout (Mr Eat Everything) because since 1959 he has been snacking on all kinds of glass and metal. He's eaten a computer, 18 bicycles, an aeroplane, 6 chandeliers, 15 supermarket trolleys, 2 beds, 7 TV sets and a pair of skis. In total, he's eaten more than 9 tonnes (1,984 pounds) of metal.

Letchemanah Ramasamy from Malaysia has pulled a double-decker bus 30 metres (around 98 feet), using only his hair.

Wim Hof of the Netherlands exposed his whole body to ice for 1 hour 8 minutes using yoga and meditation to stop himself freezing.

Meng Xu of China can thread 20 needles in his mouth using just his tongue. He did it in 6 minutes and 45 seconds in 2003.

Two people from the USA share the record for sitting in a bathtub with 75 live rattlesnakes.

The largest recorded snail was an Africa giant snail 39.3 centimetres (15.5 inches) long.

The largest tumour removed in one piece from a living person weighed 137.6 kilograms (303 pounds) and was 1 metre (3 feet) across. It weighed more than the woman it was growing inside.

The loudest recorded burp was produced by Paul Hunn of the UK in 2004. It measured nearly 105 decibels – as loud as a fast underground train whizzing past!

The largest snail ever found was 39.3 centimetres (15.5 inches) long and weighed 900 grams (2 pounds).

The largest landfill site in the world is Fresh Kills landfill, New York, USA. It is thought to contain 100 million tonnes (98 million tons) of rubbish and covers 1,200 hectares (3,000 acres).

Zafar Gill of Pakistan can lift 51.7 kilograms (113 pounds 15 ounces) of weights with a clamp attached to his right ear.

American Gary Bashaw can mix chocolate powder and milk in his mouth and pour it out of his nose as a milkshake. In 1999, he made a record-breaking 54 millilitres (1.8 ounces) of milkshake in one go.

Over a period of 40 years, American Charles Jensen had 970 operations to remove tumours (lumps), mostly from his face.

A ribbon worm washed up on the shore of Scotland in 1864 was 55 metres (180 feet) long.

Clint Hallam from New Zealand has lost the same hand (the right one) three times – in 1984 it was cut off in an accident and doctors re-attached it; it was removed again in 1989 when it got infected; a new, transplanted hand was removed in 2001 after rejection problems.

A man known as Snake Manu, from India, swallowed 200 earthworms, each at least 10 centimetres (4 inches) long, in 30 seconds in 2003.

Tom Leppard from the UK has his whole body tattooed with leopard spots, with the spaces between tattooed yellow. This makes him the most tattooed person in the world.

In 1999, Brad Byers of the USA swallowed 10 swords each 68.5 centimetres (27 inches) long, and rotated them through 180 degrees in his throat.

The noisiest spider is the European buzzing spider. The male makes a buzzing sound as it vibrates its abdomen against a leaf in order to attract a mate.

Marco Hort of Switzerland can fit 258 drinking straws in his mouth at the same time.

The fattest man in the world, Walter Hudson of New York, USA, had a waist measurement of more than 3 metres (9 feet 11 inches).

Kama Muk of the UK bravely had 600 new body piercings in a single day in 2002.

A British woman has 2,520 body piercings including a hole in her tongue large enough to poke a finger through.

The heaviest living snake is a Burmese python that weighs nearly 183 kilograms (403 pounds) and is 71 centimetres (28 inches) in width. It lives in a safari park in the USA.

Philip John has been bog-snorkelling world champion three times. In 2010 Dan Morgan set a new World Record time of 1 minute 30 seconds to swim 55 metres (60 yards) of gloopy bog.

The United States experiences more tornadoes than any other country, many of which occur in 'Tornado Alley'.

At the largest frog-leg-eating festival ever, in Florida, 2001, 13,200 people ate 3,000 kilograms (6,600 pounds) of frogs' legs fried in batter.

The longest recorded snake was a python 10 metres (35 feet 9.5 inches) long.

The carnivorous plants that devour the largest prey are from the *Nepenthacae* family. The Asian rainforest plants can digest frogs, birds and rats

Nick Thompson of the UK holds the record for eating baked beans with a cocktail stick – he ate 136 in 3 minutes.

During heart surgery in 1970, a patient with *haemophilia* (an inherited condition which stops the blood clotting) needed 1,080 litres of blood – nearly 15 baths full – as he kept bleeding.

Dean Gould of England can pick 50 winkles (a shellfish like a small snail) from shells with a pin in 1 minute, 22 seconds.